How to get from

JANUARY to DECEMBER

BOOKS BY WILL CUPPY

Maroon Tales
How to Be a Hermit
How to Tell Your Friends from the Apes
How to Become Extinct
How to Attract the Wombat
The Decline and Fall of Practically Everybody
How to Get from January to December

EDITED BY WILL CUPPY

World's Great Detective Stories
Murder Without Tears

WITH FOOTNOTES BY WILL CUPPY

Garden Rubbish & Other Country Bumps,
by Sellar & Yeatman

How to get from

ANUARY to

DECEMBER

by Will Cuppy

EDITED BY FRED FELDKAMP

DRAWINGS BY JOHN RUGE

New York HENRY HOLT AND COMPANY

Introduction

How to Get from January to December, more than any of the author's other books, gives the reader a close-up view of Cuppy, his enthusiasms, his likes and dislikes. For this book covers just about the complete range of Cuppy's interests, from astronomy to zoölogy.

Cuppy's whole life centered on those subjects. He did painstaking research endlessly on all, an occupation which ruled out the possibility of any kind of active social life. Happily, he was quite content to live the life of a hermit in his Greenwich Village apartment and at his beach shack on Jones's Island.

This staggering quantity of research was distilled into several hundred index-card-file boxes, catalogued by subject. Crammed into these boxes there are, I would estimate, some two hundred thousand cards bearing scrawled Cuppy notes —an obscure, fascinating fact; a notation on how he felt about the subject in general; relevant statements by both the famous and unheralded throughout history.

From these notes, Cuppy's posthumous works have been brought to completion. *The Decline and Fall of Practically Everybody* consumed a goodly portion of Cuppy's working time during his last sixteen years. This present book occupied him from time to time in his last fifteen years. But neither was on the point of being completed at his death. Cuppy was the insatiable researcher; there was always another volume, published in Leipzig in 1803, which might be obtainable abroad, that should be looked into before he finally got down to preparing a final draft of the chapter or piece in question.

Before his death, in September, 1949, Cuppy hoped someday to complete a number of books on which he had been working concurrently. Two of these—*The Decline and Fall of Practically Everybody* and *How to Get from January to December*—have now been published. Perhaps the others too can be completed one day.

FRED FELDKAMP

New York, N. Y.

How to get from
JANUARY to DECEMBER

JANUARY

January 1

YOU'RE wrong if you think January 1 has always been New Year's Day in English-speaking countries. William the Conqueror found the English starting the year on December 25 and ordered them to shift to January 1, probably because he had himself crowned on that day. After his time, however, the English took to celebrating on March 25, and it was hundreds of years before it got straightened out again. Most of Europe adopted January 1 with the Gregorian Calendar in 1582, but Germany, Denmark, and Sweden held out until about 1700 and England didn't make up its mind to join them until 1752. It doesn't pay to rush into these things. To me it seems perfectly clear that the year should start on January 1, but some people can't see it.

January 2

GENERAL James Wolfe, British military hero, was born in Westerham, Kent, on January 2, 1727. He captured Quebec in 1759, which is one of the main reasons why Canada doesn't belong to the French any more. While sailing down the St. Lawrence toward the Heights of Abraham the night before the battle General Wolfe recited to his officers Thomas Gray's *Elegy Written in a Country Churchyard,* and then remarked: "Gentlemen, I would rather have written that poem than take Quebec tomorrow." He is said to have admired especially the sadder parts of the elegy, such as "The paths of glory lead but to the grave." Personally, I prefer the opening line, "The lowing herds tra-la-la o'er the lea," or something of the sort. Anyway, it's one of my favorite poems.

January 3

"DEAR SIR: My husband has a dry scalp and I want him to take an egg shampoo. What do you advise?
"Subscriber"

If that is all that's wrong with your husband why not let well enough alone? But since you insist, add a cupful of warm water to the yolks of four eggs and induce him in some way to rub the mixture into his scalp. If he does this the battle is won, because naturally he'll want to get rid of the stuff as soon as possible, thus completing the treatment. Rinse with warm water, as hot water has a tendency to curdle what is left of the

eggs, and nobody wants to go around in that condition. After he has dried and combed his hair, watch him like a hawk for several days or he will attempt to wash his head with good old soap and water to get rid of that eggy feeling. I don't believe you can work it, but you probably know your man.

January 4

THESE are fine evenings for brushing up on Sirius, the Dog Star, which you'll find about three blocks below the constellation of Orion—the three diagonal stars of Orion's belt point right to it. You can't miss Sirius, because it's the brightest star in the sky, at least in the northern hemisphere. Sirius isn't such great shakes for a fixed star, being only 25 times as luminous as the Sun. It's so bright because it's so near us—only 8.8 light years distant. Rigel in Orion is supposed to be 18,000 times as luminous as the Sun, but it's 190 light years away from us. Oh, that's nothing to brag of, for they say M 31, the spiral nebula in Andromeda, is 870,000 light years away. They also say that every time a star blinks it makes a difference to each of us, so powerful are the laws of cause and effect. It may make a difference to *you*.

January 5

COMMODORE Stephen Decatur, U.S.N., was the fellow who said, "My country! In her intercourse with foreign nations, may she ever be right; but right or wrong, my country!" He said this at a dinner at Norfolk, Virginia, shortly after he had returned from fighting the corsairs in Algiers, Tunis, and Tripoli, and the next day people began picking on him and they haven't stopped yet. One of the most acute criticisms is the following, got off by Mr. G. K. Chesterton: "'My country, right or wrong,' is a thing that no patriot would think of saying except in a desperate case. It is like saying, 'My mother, drunk or sober.'" Well, Decatur always did whatever he was told to do, though maybe he didn't always know just what to say about it afterwards. And that reminds me, he was born in Sinnepuxent, Maryland, on January 5, 1779.

January 6

"DEAR SIR: Is it still considered fashionable to eat prunes?
"Wondering"

When I was young, people set great store by soaking prunes every night before going to bed. In recent years, I've never craved more than one prune at a time, and it seems kind of silly to soak one prune. The game is hardly worth the candle.

You might check with the leading prune authorities—W. F. Wight, author of *Native American Species of Prunes* and J. A. Balmer, author of *Prunes*. They'd know, if anybody would.

January 7

YOU needn't stop complaining about the humidity just because it's winter, only you'd better shift your ground. Since it's the combination of humidity and heat that displeases most people, you won't get far in cold weather by remarking, "Isn't the humidity awful?" Either get a new remark altogether or complain about the *lack* of humidity in the house. The moisture content of the atmosphere in heated rooms is frequently far below normal, so you may get some response. You can correct the low humidity of your home by balancing shallow pans of water on radiators and other unlikely spots. Or you can increase the humidity by reducing the temperature. You will then be a little chilly, but the humidity will be normal.

9

January 8

BRILLAT-SAVARIN, the eminent gourmet, once wrote: "Tell me what a man eats and I'll tell you the kind of a man he is."

That's true enough. Show me a man who eats *pêches au Chablis* and I can tell you some stories about him that will make your hair curl.

Brillat-Savarin also set down an account of a breakfast for three which lasted from 10 A.M. until 8 P.M.

"The destiny of nations," he wrote at another point, "depends on the manner wherein they take their food." Oh, sure! If they live on *pêches au Chablis* and spend ten hours over breakfast, some nation that lives on raw dog meat comes along and licks the living bejeezus out of them. Destiny, indeed!

Most gourmets have money and high blood-pressure. To me they will always be misguided men who starve snails, drown ortolans in brandy, gorge geese, and gloat about it.

January 9

SIR Humphry Davy's safety-lamp for miners was successfully tried out January 9, 1816, and later on a statistician presented figures showing that in the ten years following its introduction there were more than twice as many explosions in mines as in the ten years before. That merely shows that some statisticians are like that. Sir Humphry also discovered potassium, sodium, boron, and hydrogen phosphide and made many improvements in widely varying fields. In 1823 he found that if you render the copper sheathing of ships negatively electrical by adding some zinc or copper strips the copper will stop corroding but will quickly become so covered with seaweed and shellfish that you have to take the strips off again. Speaking of economics, Sir Humphry once said: "Riches appear to me not at all necessary; but competence, I think, is." And there's the rub.

January 10

ETHAN ALLEN, Revolutionary soldier and hero of Vermont, was born at Litchfield, Connecticut, in 1739, on guess what day of what month. Right—January 10. He got up the Green Mountain Boys, you know. He called upon Fort Ticonderoga to surrender in 1775, and when the British asked him by whose authority he said, "In the name of the Great Jehovah and the Continental Congress!" Naturally, the British surrendered. Ethan Allen is sometimes called the liberator of Vermont, though just what he liberated it from I don't know. Anyway, there's a very nice statue of him in the State House at Montpelier, Vermont. In his *Literary History of the American Revolution,* Mr. M. C. Tyler states that Ethan was "a blustering frontier hero—an able-minded ignoramus of rough and ready humor, of boundless self-confidence," and so forth. I have gone rather thoroughly into the matter and I find no statues of Mr. Tyler *anywhere.*

January 11

SUPPOSING you met a bear in the woods, William James, distinguished American philosopher and psychologist, said that first (a) you see the bear, then (b) you run, then (c) you are frightened. That is hard to explain to some people because they always ask you what made you run. A Mr. Marshall Dunn, who once encountered a bear near Black Oak Lake, Wisconsin, states that (a) he saw the bear eating

huckleberries in the bushes, (b) was definitely frightened, (c) shot at the bear and missed it, (d) was still more frightened, and (e) ran and got a farmer to shoot the bear. But by that time the bear had gone and the farmer didn't believe there ever had *been* a bear. Come to think of it, William James was born in New York City on January 11, 1842.

January 12

THIS is the birthday of Edmund Burke, one of the greatest orators Great Britain ever produced. He was born in Dublin, probably on January 12, 1729, and began to talk at an extremely early age. I like a good speech myself, but I think it can be overdone. For instance, in his impeachment of Warren Hastings, Governor-General of India, for high crimes and misdemeanors, Burke seldom stopped talking for about eight hours. At the end of that time the House of Commons acquitted Hastings by a large majority. During this trial he once asked the celebrated Doctor Samuel Parr whether he had liked his speech. "No, Edmund," replied Doctor Parr. "It was oppressed by metaphor, dislocated by parentheses, and debilitated by amplification." That's about my attitude.

January 13

"DEAR SIR: Is it true that certain foods make some people feel amorous?

"*Bachelor*"

They say that about a number of edibles, but don't get your hopes up. I've been eating the items in question—potatoes, onions, celery, caviar, oysters, and other shellfish—for years, and I feel about as usual.

However, you might think about what Brillat-Savarin said about the truffle: "The truffle is not a positive aphrodisiac, but it may under certain circumstances render women more affectionate and men more amiable."

Truffles are globose, whatever that is—brown, black, sandy, and warty. The taste of truffles has been likened variously to that of strawberries, garlic, flannel, and unclassified. Some pâté de foie gras contains truffles.

Or you could try amassing a great deal of money. That works fine.

January 14

WHEN life seems dull and drab I often think that if I could only get a good look at Halley's Comet it would make all the difference. Edmund Halley, of course, did not invent the comet himself. But he observed it in 1682, decided that it was the same comet that came about every seventy-six years, and predicted that it would show up again in 1758 or 1759, which it did.

Mr. Halley didn't live to see his figures verified, I'm sorry to say. In fact, he passed away on January 14, 1742.

January 15

LOUIS XIV of France was a patron of literature. That is, he did not care for literature himself, but he would find out which authors were considered the best and then he would give them enough to encourage them but not enough to spoil them. When he was feeling especially artistic, he would treat Racine and Corneille almost as his equals. A couple of his favorite authors starved to death in the excitement, but Louis XIV thought so well of Molière, the great comic dramatist, that he appointed him his *valet de chambre,* with the privilege of making the royal bed. Molière did not starve to death, but his funeral was very sketchy and nobody knows where he was buried. Louis XIV, however, was buried at St. Denis. You can't lose him. As I started to say, this is Molière's birthday. He was born January 15, 1622.

January 16

ON THIS date in 1930 a number of things happened. It rained in Salt Lake City and snowed in Denver and Professor Franz Oberth of Budapest, who was making a rocket to fly to the moon, temporarily stopped work, for lack of funds. Former President Coolidge consented to write a five-hundred-word inscription to be engraved on Mount Rushmore, and President and Mrs. Hoover gave a dinner at the White House for Vice President Curtis and a good time was had by all— at least the papers said so. King Feisal of Iraq arranged a conference with Ibn Saud of the Nejd, and from Little America, Antarctica, Rear Admiral Byrd sent a radio message which turned on a light over a bust of Benjamin Franklin in Philadelphia. And what were *you* doing—just marking time?

January 17

"DEAR SIR: Whatever became of Thrift Week, which used to begin on January 17, and what are your suggestions?
"Worried"

There is still a Thrift Week, but some of us aren't going to do much about it. I have never had enough money to keep track of, let alone be thrifty with, so it would be rather silly of me to celebrate Thrift Week. I got busy on your account, though, and called up some people who used to disseminate Thrift Week programs. They said they had nothing to report and that I might call up a Mr. X, who had taken over their share of the matter. So I called up Mr. X and he was out. Why don't you celebrate by tying some nickels in the corner of your handkerchief, *Worried*? If you do this whenever you have a spare nickel, some day when you are in financial straits you will find that you have three or four nickels.

January 18

SOME of us aren't as dumb as we look and some of us are about what you'd expect. I am far from satisfied with my own features, but taking it by and large I wouldn't trade with Daniel Webster, whose birthday we celebrate today—he was born January 18, 1782, at Salisbury, New Hampshire. He impressed Mrs. Nathaniel Hawthorne this way: "The front of Jove, the regal, commanding air which cleared a path before him, the voice of thunder and music, the unfathomable eye—all these external signs said, 'Here is a Great Man!'"

No, it's too much responsibility. Besides, somebody would always be making remarks. For instance, Thomas Carlyle said of Webster: "God Almighty never created a man half as wise as he looks." See how it works?

January 19

JAMES WATT, inventor of the modern steam-engine, was born on January 19, 1736, at Greenock, Renfrewshire, Scotland. When he was fifteen years old, his aunt, Mrs. Muirhead, reproved him for watching the steam come out of the tea kettle instead of reading a book. This teaches us to be careful about reproving a boy who appears to be idle. He may be inventing something, but the chances are that he isn't. Watt's steam-engine drove machinery of all kinds and his ideas were later applied to the locomotive. I can't get very excited about the steam-engine, but I know I should, because the steam-engine has played a great part in making civilization what it is today. Thanks largely to James Watt and inventors like him, our transportation has improved so wonderfully that

you can hardly go across the street without getting run over, and lots of people think that's just fine.

January 20

I HAVE nothing against mice, in moderation. If you have mice, I hope you're keeping them out of drafts and damp places, as they are sensitive in these respects and a sudden drop in temperature might prove fatal. Give them a few oats and some cod-liver oil now and then, and above all don't feed them cheese—it overheats their blood and upsets their basal metabolism.

My own mice just eat whatever I have in the place, including soap. Not an ideal diet, but they'll have to make it do or move elsewhere.

January 21

ALL babies born from now until midnight of February 19 will be under the Sign of Aquarius, the Water-Bearer. They will be lucky, too, for Aquarius persons are always better than middling. Many of them are geniuses, though here and there you'll find one who's a little slow on the uptake. Aquarius persons of the past and present include Franklin D. Roosevelt, Abraham Lincoln, George Jean Nathan, Susan B. Anthony, Maxine Elliott, Li Hung Chang, Charles M. Schwab, John D. Rockefeller, Jr., Adelina Patti, Zebulon Montgomery Pike, Lord Byron, Charles Lutwidge Dodgson, Ole Bull, Havelock Ellis, John Barrymore, Thomas A. Edison, and Frederick the Great. Never argue with Aquarius persons. They seem to know all the answers.

January 22

"DEAR SIR: Is it true that Lord Byron, my favorite poet, put his hair up in curl-papers?
"Disillusioned"

You're positively uncanny, *Disillusioned,* the way you always connect with somebody's birthday. Do you do it on purpose, or didn't you know that Lord Byron was born in London on January 22, 1788? Yes, it seems to be a fact that Byron's beautiful brown ringlets were manufactured by means of papillotes, or paper curlers, so what? It was his own hair, wasn't it? I don't think this need make any difference between you and Byron if you really love his poems. A poet's personal eccentricities do not necessarily affect his work. For instance, I know a poet who carries a cane and it doesn't seem to affect his poems at all. If he didn't carry a cane, they'd still be terrible.

TODAY'S birthday honors go to John Hancock, the first man to sign the Declaration of Independence. John Hancock was born January 23, 1737, in what is now Quincy, Massachusetts. He was graduated from Harvard, at the age of seventeen, and just how much he knew at that time I shouldn't

like to say. He inherited a lot of money and became a rich merchant and finally took to stirring people up against the Stamp Act and that sort of thing. So when the day came to sign the Declaration of Independence, he stepped up and wrote his name about three times as big as anyone else, remarking as he did so: "There, I guess King George will be able to read that!" It would be very nice to have John Hancock's autograph, but I'd just as soon have one of Button Gwinnett's. Button Gwinnett's autographs are worth about $25,000 apiece if you want one and about nothing if you don't.

January 24

IF AN animal does something they call it instinct. If we do exactly the same thing for the same reason they call it intelligence.

Entomologists say that ants, for example, are guided entirely by instinct and not by intelligence. They say the ants do not know what they are doing. And do the entomologists know what *they* are doing? Besides watching ants, I mean. I'm only asking.

I guess what they mean is that we all make mistakes, but intelligence enables us to do it on purpose.

That's all very well, but *I* believe the toad is thinking as he sits there, perfectly still. He *must* be.

January 25

ROBERT BURNS, ace of Scottish poets, was born in a humble cot at Alloway on January 25, 1759. I got off on the wrong foot with Burns, as I was practically brought up on the following lines, quoted and requoted to me by my mother:

> O wad some power the giftie gie us
> To see oursels as ithers see us!
> It wad frae monie a blunder free us
>   And foolish notion.

Naturally, I got the idea that this Robert Burns was somebody who had made a special study of my looks and other weaknesses and was trying his best to get me down. In after-life I read some of Burns myself and came to the conclusion that maybe he had been right about me. It didn't help much, though, when I discovered that the lines which had harried my childhood days were a part of the poem entitled *To a Louse*.

January 26

THINGS were humming on this date in 1927. There was trouble in China. It was three degrees above zero in New York City, 39 below in Brainerd, Minnesota, and 48 above in Los Angeles. John D. Rockefeller whistled and danced a jig when he played eight holes of golf in 47 at Ormond Beach, Florida. The Duke and Duchess of York sailed for Australia after spending the day in Panama City, and word from Paris indicated that spring styles would stress light green, cochineal, red banana, silvery gray, and light purplish blue. President Coolidge asked for an appropriation of $185,000 to install some ventilating and dehumidizing machinery in the Senate Chamber, as many senators had complained that after a day in the Senate they felt very much depressed. And no wonder.

January 27

"DEAR SIR: Where can I reach that fellow who's going to Mars in a rocket?

"Al"

I advise you to investigate the whole subject pretty thoroughly before you undertake a trip to Mars with that fellow or anyone else. It may sound old-fashioned, but we were never intended to go to Mars in a rocket, and that's the long and short of it, Al.

The only thing I like about Mars is that the gravitational pull there is so slight that one could jump three times as high as one can on earth, but that would hardly be worth the trip. I suppose the novelty would soon wear off.

Why not content yourself with signalling to Mars? I don't say your signals would ever reach Mars, and if they did the

Martians would be little the wiser. Naturally, they wouldn't know what you meant by your signals or what to do about it—I wouldn't know myself. If there aren't any Martians, that wouldn't help much, either.

Well, so long, *Al*.

January 28

EDWARD VI, the son of Henry VIII and Jane Seymour, became King of England and Ireland at the age of nine years upon the death of his father on January 28, 1547. He was a frail and rather useless youth, the only uninteresting Tudor in all history. He died in his sixteenth year and was buried in his grandfather's chapel in Westminster Abbey and that was the end of him. There's a gentleman in California who claimed that poor little Edward VI didn't die, but lived on in disguise, possibly under the name of Sir Francis Bacon, and as such wrote Shakespeare's plays. I try to keep an open mind on these things, but I can see two weaknesses in our friend's theory. In the first place, Edward VI did nothing of the sort. Secondly, Shakespeare wrote his own plays. If he didn't it was somebody else of the same name.

January 29

ANOTHER way to kill time is to study the beautiful geometrical forms of snowflakes, all of which are different, just like the rest of us. Most snowflakes are triangular or hexagonal, since water is composed of two parts of hydrogen and one of oxygen, but exactly why that should produce triangles and hexagons has slipped my mind for the moment. The late Mr. W. A. Bentley, of Jericho, Vermont, photographed more than five thousand snowflakes, and only a fraction of them were perfect, so snowflakes have their own troubles. Our American snow is very beautiful, but some people prefer the delicately tinted snow on the Alps. This is caused by billions and billions of tinted bacteria, but that makes no difference to the true Alpine fan. He will spend his last cent to go over and look at them. American bacteria aren't good enough.

January 30

SEEMS that the English beheaded King Charles I for one thing or another, and there were people who talked about nothing else for years. Whatever the conversation, they would manage to drag in King Charles's head. King Charles's head is no longer regarded as a good subject of conversation, because very few people would know what you were talking about, although that also applies to most other subjects of conversation. Besides, it doesn't really matter any more, for King Charles would be gone now, anyway. Here and there some old fogy will bring up the subject because he can't think of anything else, and once in a blue moon somebody will mention it because there's a good reason for doing so. For instance, Charles I was beheaded on January 30, 1649.

January 31

"DEAR SIR: Why on earth don't you ever write about Scotch proverbs?"

"Constant R."

Funny, I just bought a book of Scotch proverbs, and I was wondering what to do with it. My own view is that Scotch

23

proverbs are often a little vague to outsiders, since one can't see the sense for the Scotch. For example: *Better thole a grumph than a sumph*. That doubtless expresses a high grade of wisdom, painfully arrived at by those who have tholed sumphs, perhaps through no fault of their own, only to discover when it is too late that they were the grumph type all along. Again: *If a man's gaun doon the brae ilka ane gies him a jundie*. I have a strange feeling that I've been through that very thing myself, but I'll never be sure. How do you feel about it?

FEBRUARY

February 1

I DON'T know why it is, but somebody is always picking on February. In the first place, February was invented by the Roman king Numa Pompilius, if there ever was such a person. He gave it only twenty-nine days, except in leap year, when there were thirty, and the extra day was sandwiched in between February 23 and February 24 to make it harder. Numa also placed February at the end of the year, but later on it was put where it belonged. Then Augustus took one of February's days and added it to August just to be doing something, and long afterwards February 29 was dropped in such years as 1800 and 1900, where the first two numerals are not divisible by four, or some such nonsense.

And the next time someone wants a little publicity he'll do something to February. A good many people think February is our worst month. The truth is that February would be all right if they would only let it alone.

February 2

THE woodchuck, or ground-hog, is a brownish North American rodent with very peculiar habits. In a wild state he lives on grass, clover, lettuce, and cabbage, but in captivity he prefers bread and milk. He would probably like to have bread and milk all the time but he can't get it. Along in November, after storing some fat under his skin, he crawls into his burrow and goes to sleep until about seven or eight o'clock on the morning of February 2, when he brushes his whiskers and emerges from his home to forecast the weather. If the day is cloudy and cold, he decides that the winter is over, but if the sun is shining brightly and it feels kind of warm he says it's still winter and goes back to sleep for another six weeks, all of which proves that he has no sense whatever. Or it may be that the ground-hog has no such ideas at all, as he is only a lower vertebrate, and lower vertebrates can't think up things like that. Those who can are called higher vertebrates.

February 3

THIS is as good a time as any to start thinking about Collop Monday, so called from the old English custom of eating col-

lops, or pieces of salted meat and eggs, as a sort of preparation for Shrove Tuesday, or Pancake Day, when everybody would switch to pancakes. After eating all the collops they could get, the boys of the village would go around singing the following song:

> *Shrovetide is near at hand,*
> *And I be come a shroving;*
> *Pray, dame, something—*
> *An apple or a dumpling.*

Most of these boys grew up and became the ancestors of thousands of people alive today, and yet you wonder why things are the way they are.

February 4

"DEAR SIR: I have an aunt who constantly uses the word *Mondayish*. How can I break her of this habit?
"*Worried*"

Observe your aunt closely for a month or so, and you will probably find that she uses the word *Mondayish* only on Mondays as part of her weekly announcement that she feels Mondayish. If so, she is speaking English and is clearly within her rights, although some authorities might accuse her of looseness. *The New English Dictionary* thus defines *Mondayish*: "Affected with the indisposition often felt by clergymen on Monday, resulting from the work of Sunday."

I think this may easily be stretched to include aunts and, in some instances, other persons as well. Of course, if your aunt feels Mondayish on *Tuesday* she is going a little too far and should try some good standard tonic.

February 5

ONCE there was a little boy named Zebulon Montgomery Pike. He was born at Lamington, New Jersey, on February 5, 1779, and was named Zebulon because his father was named Zebulon—those things seem to run in some families. Zebulon is in the Bible, and I am sure you know all about it. Young Zebulon became a soldier and explorer, and in 1805 he found what he thought was the source of the Mississippi, but wasn't. The next year he discovered Pike's Peak, which is a mountain of the Rampart range of the Rockies, in El Paso County, Colorado, 14,108 feet high. He failed to reach the summit, but afterwards several millions of people reached it by horse, cog-railway, and automobile. In the Gay Nineties you were simply nobody, socially, unless you had been to the summit of Pike's Peak on the cog-railway. Nowadays this is more or less optional. Society is not what it used to be.

P.S.—Some say Zebulon was born on January 5, but I was told February 5, and I'm sticking to it.

February 6

"DEAR SIR: I have more money than I know what to do with and should like your advice on period furniture. I already have a William and Mary chest.

"Distracted"

I have written you a long letter, *Distracted*. Meanwhile, I suggest that you try the Queen Anne style, which comes next after William and Mary. As Queen Anne was almost as large as William and Mary together, the furniture of her day was much stronger and inclined to curvilinear outlines—William and Mary were more rectangular. The Queen Anne style also includes cabriole legs, which are not nearly so bad as they sound. If you are in earnest, you could even go in for ball-and-claw feet, unless you prefer bracket feet or thimble feet. By a strange coincidence, Queen Anne was born February 6, 1665.

February 7

I SEE where some British scientists are wondering why whales do not get the bends after diving to great depths and ascending rapidly to the surface. It's none of my business, in a way, but since we are here to help others I don't mind telling them. The animals in question do not get the bends simply because they are whales and whales do not get the bends. The scientists have doubtless heard that whales are mammals and have drawn the hasty conclusion that they are therefore practically human beings, and that, after diving to a depth of 328 feet and staying down fifteen minutes they should take about an hour and a half to return to the surface in order to prevent a too violent release of nitrogen from their blood. In my opinion, all this fuss comes from classifying whales as mammals in the first place. I knew somebody would get it all mixed up.

February 8

GENERAL William Tecumseh Sherman was born at Lancaster, Ohio, on February 8, 1820, and we all know what he said about war, although he could never remember having said it. Anyway, he finally marched through Georgia and a Mr. Work wrote a song about it, and everywhere General Sherman went somebody was sure to sing it or play it or both. Once when he was in Dublin, writing some letters in his hotel room, he heard a band coming up the street playing *Marching Through Georgia*, so he dashed to his trunk, put on his uniform, assumed a patient expression, and sat down to wait. Well, the band went right past the hotel and faded away in the distance, for it turned out that the tune of *Marching Through Georgia* is an old Irish favorite and there was a picnic that day. All right, then, *you* tell one.

February 9

IF YOU care much about the stars of the heavens you'd better get busy about Nova Herculis, which was discovered not very long ago by a man in England and also by Robert A. Lewis, a seventeen-year-old newsboy of Columbia, South Carolina. According to the astronomers, Nova Herculis is the result of a terrific explosion that took place in the constellation Hercules about 1,300 years ago. The astronomers know that because astronomers know those things. It's rather urgent, as something else may happen up there any minute, and you might as well be in on the ground floor. Almost anybody can find Vega and the head of Draco, with the aid of a map or a star-gazer—look right between them and you have Nova Herculis. You should get a very good view around 5 A.M. If you can see nothing at all, at least you're up bright and early.

February 10

"DEAR SIR: Why do you keep harping on mystery characters who stare, whether at one another, at inanimate objects, or even into space, the last of which seems to make you especially furious. Why shouldn't they stare if they want to?
                                    "Anonymous"

I am just a fellow who does not like the constant use of the verb "to stare" in mysteries or anywhere else. What's wrong with the verb "to look"? This staring business, *Anonymous,* is the worst cliché I have encountered in a long and checkered career, and I was only trying to stop it, that's all.

As for staring into space—or more frequently staring *blankly* into space—as so many mystery heroines do most of the time, I object to it on the ground that it can't be done. According to

Webster, to stare is "to gaze or look fixedly, as through fear, wonder, surprise, impudence, etc.; to fasten an earnest and prolonged gaze on some object." I submit that you cannot do that blankly and you probably cannot do it into space at all, because where is the object in that case? Try it some time, *Anonymous,* if you can find any space. But watch out for the man with the net. He might not understand.

February 11

AND that reminds me of Aristides the Just, the Athenian statesman, with whose life story you are doubtless familiar, and I wish I could say the same. Aristides the Just is still holding his own in the encyclopedia, and he receives honorable mention once in a while when there's nothing else to mention; but nobody seems to know when the poor man was born, unless it was maybe somewhere around 530 B.C. So far all efforts to provide him with a definite birthday have failed. Why wouldn't it be a good plan to put him down for February 11, 530 B.C. and get it off our minds, so that we can go about our business without *that* hanging over us? Oh, yes —one of the Athenians who helped banish Aristides the Just said that he had nothing against him except that he was sick and tired of hearing him called Aristides the Just. That was very wrong of the Athenian, but I know how he felt. Those things do get on one's nerves.

February 12

BESIDES Abraham Lincoln, eminent persons born on February 12 include Charles Darwin, George Meredith, Peter Cooper, James Dwight Dana, and Tadeusz Andrzej Bona-

wentura Kosciuszko—Thaddeus Kosciusko to you. Kosciusko was born in 1746 at Mereczowszczyno, Poland, and left there as soon as he could. He fought in our Revolutionary War, went back home, and fell, severely wounded, in the struggle for Polish independence in 1794, but he recovered and lived until 1817, part of the time in Philadelphia.

Thomas Campbell wrote the poem containing the famous line,

> *And Freedom shrieked as Kosciusko fell!*

And Coleridge, for some reason or other, also exclaimed in a sonnet on Kosciusko,

> *O what a loud and fearful shriek was there!*

Excellent as both these poems are, there seems to have been no actual necessity for so much shrieking. The general effect, moreover, has been unfortunate, as a great many people now have the impression that it was Kosciusko who shrieked. Well, he didn't.

35

February 13

TODAY'S birthday honors might as well go to Charles Maurice de Talleyrand-Périgord, French diplomat and wise-cracker, who arrived on February 12 or 13, 1754—use your own judgment. Talleyrand's *mots* were regarded as hot in his day, but if I should tell you a lot of them you would say they were only so-so, and you would be right. He is famous for remarking to Napoleon, after the Battle of Leipzig: "It seems to me, sire, to be the beginning of the end."

I had an uncle once who remarked: "It seems to me, sire, to be the end of the beginning," but he never got into any collection of *mots*. Talleyrand also said: "Mistrust first impulses, they are always good"—which is feeble and foolish and phony from any point of view. By the way, I wish Mr. Burton Stevenson, author of *The Home Book of Quotations*, had found out who invented the epigram "I love red roses, they are so yellow!" I heard it years ago, and it still worries me.

February 14

LOTS of people will be getting valentines today, and others may meditate upon the end of Captain James Cook, English explorer, who perished in a brush with the natives of Hawaii on February 14, 1779, leaving a widow (*née* Batts) in strait-ened circumstances. Captain Cook made three voyages to the South Seas and thereabouts, mapped a good deal of the Pacific, discovered numerous islands, annexed them to Great Britain, and generally brought untold wealth to his country. After his second voyage he was rewarded with a beautiful speech of thanks, a gold medal, and a job in Greenwich Hospital. If he had returned from his last trip he would probably have received some actual cash, at least that was the rumor.

This teaches that we should all work very hard, and if anything comes of it so much the better. Although Captain Cook was a great and good man we don't get excited about him any more. I wouldn't have looked him up, even, but I thought he was a pirate.

February 15

"DEAR SIR: I see where the Big Dipper is breaking up and will be an entirely different shape in about 50,000 years. Is there nothing we can depend on?
                                                                "Disgusted"

No, there isn't, *Disgusted,* if you come right down to it. You must try to realize that nothing stays put forever and act accordingly. It is true that the five central stars of the Big Dipper are rushing toward the sun at eight or ten miles a second and that eventually the Big Dipper will look like something else. This will be tough on people whose only interest in life is something the shape of a dipper, but there is a brighter side to the picture.

The real name of the Big Dipper is Ursa Major, or the Greater Bear, and my hope is that in 50,000 years it will look a lot more like what it's supposed to be. Whatever happens, it couldn't look *less* like a bear than it does at present. Long, long ago, when Ursa Major was named, bears probably looked more like dippers than they do today. You can't depend on bears, either.

February 16

ON THIS date in 1929 the thermometer registered 24 degrees below zero in Winnipeg and 80 above in Miami. President-elect and Mrs. Hoover were entertained at a luncheon party at Palm Beach, the decorations being red roses, white lilacs, and blue delphiniums. King Alfonso of Spain had a little spat with Premier Primo de Rivera, and five thousand bottles of beer exploded in Berka, Thuringia. In London, Sir Arthur Keith, lecturing before the Royal College of Surgeons, said the human brain resembled a newspaper office, and I wish I knew just how he meant that.

February 17

"DEAR SIR: I may go to Cornwall some time, so how can I learn the Cornish language?

"*Ambitious*"

You're a little late, *Ambitious*, as the Cornish language became extinct about the middle of the eighteenth century. It belonged to the Brythonic group of the Celtic division of the Indo-European languages, and the inhabitants of Cornwall finally decided they'd had enough of that sort of thing. The last person to speak Cornish fluently seems to have been Mrs. Dorothy Pentreath, a fishwife of Mousehole, near Penzance, who used to swear something awful at people who came to hear her speak Cornish—at least, it sounded like swearing. If you go to Cornwall, *Ambitious*, just be yourself. Or why don't you take up numerology?

February 18

THREE cheers for Alessandro Volta, Italian physicist, who was born at Como on February 18, 1745. Volta invented the

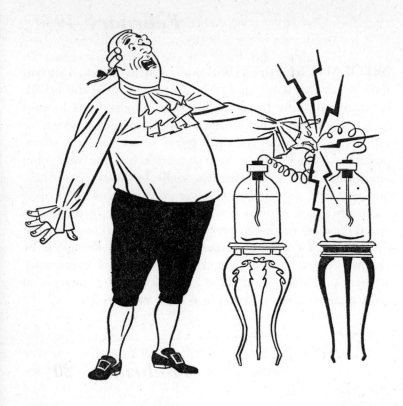

Voltaic pile, an apparatus for developing electric currents by chemical action, and volts were named after him as soon as it was generally realized that there *were* volts. In electrical science the volt, properly so called, as distinguished from the ohm and the ampere—that is to say, a long technical discussion of the volt would be out of place here, even if I were better acquainted with the subject.

I am no Volta, but I have always been interested in electrical problems. For instance, why is it that whenever I, personally, plug in a bridge lamp or other gadget, at home or abroad, there is a slight fizzing sound and all the lights in the house go out? Why does it always have to be me? Why not somebody else for a change?

February 19

NIKOLAUS KOPPERNIGK was born in Thorn, Prussian Poland, on February 19, 1473, and proved to be the brightest member of the Koppernigk family. Under his Latinized name, Copernicus, he invented the Copernican system of astronomy, which has the earth going around the sun, in opposition to the Ptolemaic system, which had the sun going around the earth. Copernicus was right, but some people held out for a long time and some never even heard of the Copernican system, as education was not compulsory in those days and there were no newspapers or radio. In our times the latest findings of science are carried to all parts of the globe by countless agencies and dinned into the ears of every man, woman, and child. And there are still heated arguments in some quarters about whether or not the world is flat.

February 20

IF YOU were born anywhere from February 20 through March 21, you are under the Sign of Pisces, the Fishes. Pisces persons are neither cold-blooded nor especially fond of fish. Pisces ladies are mostly beautiful and gifted, often taking up art, but they are afraid of mice and inclined to think they have left the electric heater burning. Many Pisces men are just great big boys at heart. They frequently excel as financiers, botanists, firemen, and sculptors. Celebrated Pisces persons of history include Cardinal Newman, Enrico Caruso, Edna St. Vincent Millay, Michelangelo, Grover Cleveland, Frederic Chopin, Christopher Marlowe, George Washington, Amelia Bingham, Ellen Terry, Augustus Saint-Gaudens, Leo XIII, William Jennings Bryan, Victor Hugo, Percy A. Rockefeller, Amerigo Vespucci, Geraldine Farrar, Henrik Ibsen, Luther

Burbank, Oswald Garrison Villard, and Ludwig II of Bavaria. Want to make something of it?

February 21

"DEAR SIR: How would you use the word *ineluctable* in a sentence, and what does it mean, anyhow?
"Doting Mother"

I should not hesitate to use it in practically any sentence, if I felt in the mood. For instance, "You're looking very ineluctable today," or "This is certainly an ineluctable piece of pie I seem to be eating." The last thing you need worry about is what ineluctable *means*, because there are only a chosen few who know and your chance of meeting any of them is only about one in 3,462,587. If you want to be quite safe, however, I recommend the sentence, "Some things are positively ineluctable." Let me know how you make out.

February 22

ACCORDING to Parson Weems, who heard it from an old lady who said she was a distant relative of all concerned, George Washington's exact words that time were these: "I can't tell a lie, pa; you know I can't tell a lie. I did cut it with my hatchet." And the elder Washington spoke precisely as follows: "Run to my arms, you dearest boy, run to my arms; glad am I, George, that you killed my tree, for you have paid me for it a thousand-fold. Such an act of heroism in my son is worth more than a thousand trees, though blossomed with silver and their fruits of the purest gold."

41

Parson Weems' story led to an epidemic of mutilated cherry trees and little boys with hatchets who ate off the mantelpiece for a day or two. One of these little boys thought it over and announced that either Parson Weems or the old lady was lying, and that is about where the matter stands at present.

February 23

SPEAKING of art, here's to George Frederick Watts, English painter and sculptor, who was born in London on February 23, 1817. Unless I'm losing my memory, Watts painted that bare-footed young lady who is sitting on what appears to be the world, with her eyes bandaged, holding in her arms a harp that has only one string left and is otherwise in a bad state of repair. The name of the picture is *Hope*. I never could understand why. If she still hopes to play that one-stringed harp, in her condition, she is a victim of misplaced confidence. In fact, I have never seen a young lady whose general outlook seemed to be more hopeless. Yes, we had a copy of *Hope* at home. We were right there with a Barye lion, too.

February 24

ONE meets some peculiar people around, and not in the circus. Just when you're beginning to think pretty well of people, you run across somebody who puts sugar on sliced tomatoes.

There are people who hum at concerts. This shows that they know the tune. (That isn't all it shows.) There are people who keep their money. There are people who would give you their last nickel if they had it themselves.

There are people you wouldn't believe.

February 25

"DEAR SIR: Do you believe that the way to a man's heart is through his tummy? And is it true that there are certain foods which will make a man propose almost instantly?

"*Lonely*"

My answer to both questions would be Yes and No. The lowdown on almost any question, *Lonely*, is that it all depends. As for foods which cause the male to forget himself, very favorable results are often obtained with strawberry shortcake. I knew a fellow once who proposed to seventeen girls the same summer just on account of their shortcake. The strawberries were wonderful that year. Perhaps I should add that the shortcake must be made of biscuit dough, shortened with butter. Some men like it made of sponge-cake, but I do not believe you would find permanent happiness with such persons. You'd only be wasting sponge-cake. By the way, strawberries are in market now, so if things seem drab you have only yourself to blame.

February 26

YOUR old friend William F. Cody, alias Buffalo Bill, was born in Scott County, Iowa, on February 26, 1846. He won his nickname by shooting nearly five thousand buffaloes in 1867, when he was employed by the Kansas Pacific Railway to provide meat for its workers. Some say that Buffalo Bill never shot any buffaloes whatever, but I can testify that he shot plenty of clay pigeons and glass balls with a shotgun said to be loaded with buckshot. Others say that he caused the buffaloes to become practically extinct, and that isn't true, either. There were about five million buffaloes in those days

and he merely scratched the surface. What really happened to the buffaloes is just what you might expect if you've ever seen one in a zoo. The moths got into them.

February 27

SOME day an interesting book should be written about the decline and fall of the whisker in modern poetry. The facts are all in now, so why doesn't somebody add them up and try to sell them? The Victorian school of heavily bearded verse, starting with Lord Tennyson and Browning, produced some pretty dire results, taking it by and large. In America we still feel the effects of Bryant, Whittier, Longfellow—yes, and

Whitman—all of whom appear to have developed long gray beards at a comparatively early age. Now that we know so much about vitamins, it would be nice to know whether the whiskers caused the poetry to be the way it was, or *vice versa*. I just thought I'd mention it, as this is Henry Wadsworth Longfellow's birthday. He was born in Portland, Maine, on February 27, 1807.

February 28

I DON'T seem to have heard whether anything has been done lately about reforming the calendar. The plan, you know, was to fix the calendar so that the same day would fall on the same date every year, if that's the way to put it. For instance June 6 would fall on Wednesday every year, instead of Thursday, as it did in 1935, or Tuesday, as in 1933, or Sunday, as in 1875. This can be done by giving March, May, August, and December only thirty days each, instead of thirty-one, taking one day from April, stabilizing February at thirty, having a thing called Year Day between December 30 and January 1, and another thing called Leap Day right after June 30 when necessary. It might be fun.

There will be trouble, I'll bet, from people whose birthdays occur on March 31, May 31, August 31, or December 31, because there won't *be* any such dates any more. Well, those born December 31 will just have to celebrate on Year Day and like it. Besides, my own birthday is August 23. All in all I withdraw any objections I may have made to calendar reform in the past. It really looks as though it might provide a rational method of telling what day it is without going down cellar and scrabbling through a lot of old newspapers—which generally leaves you about where you were, anyway.

February 29

TODAY'S birthday honors, such as they are, go to Gioachino Antonio Rossini, Italian composer, who was born at Pesaro on February 29, 1792. Rossini fans who feel moved to celebrate his birthday have plenty of time to work up to it.

They can leave me out of it. I have nothing against Rossini, except that he wrote the music to *The Barber of Seville*, and every one of the seventeen times anybody has ever given me free tickets to the opera guess what it turned out to be—yes, *Il Barbiere di Siviglia*. Seventeen times. Now I ask you. Well, the fans can solve their problem as best they may. I've done enough for Gioachino Antonio Rossini.

MARCH

March 1

HOORAY! March is here again! Some people are not very enthusiastic about March but I couldn't do without it myself. Anyway, February's over and next month will be April. There's a bright side, you see, even to March.

As in other months, keep your mind occupied and you'll be all right. In certain parts of our country the inhabitants get through March nicely by looking for the first robin, beginning promptly at sunrise this morning and continuing until the newspapers are just one mass of robins. There is little chance that you, personally, will find the first robin, for statistics show that the bird generally appears at Winsted, Connecticut. That needn't stop you from trying.

March 2

GENERAL Sam Houston, who defeated Santa Ana that time, was born near Lexington, Virginia, on March 2, 1793. He was not, as some suppose, always killing Mexicans and shouting, "Remember the Alamo!" He was equally famous for his chivalry. He would boom, "Lady, I salute you!" whenever he met one, at the same time performing gyrations said to have resembled parts of a fencing lesson. While in Congress he spent most of his time whittling little wooden hearts, which he later presented to deserving members of the opposite sex. It is a curious fact that chronic whittlers are likely to lead very romantic lives when they are not whittling. Nobody knows whether the romance brings on the whittling or whether they just whittle between times or what.

March 3

"DEAR SIR: I wish to protest in the strongest terms against your proposed reform of the calendar. Why do you want to have thirteen months in the year, anyway?
                                                                    "Puzzled"

Some very charming people want to have thirteen months in the year, *Puzzled*, but I am not one of them. You don't know me if you think I would support any plan under which we would have to pay rent oftener than we do now. I should not regard that as a sign of progress. The new calendar I am supporting has the usual twelve months, tinkered with only a little, and the rent problem will remain right where it is at present. That is, each of us will owe exactly the same number of months' back rent we always have.

Of course, after we have changed the number of days in some of the months, we can't go around muttering "Thirty days hath September" and whatever comes next, as it won't agree with the facts. We'll have to make it "Thirty-one days hath January, July, and October" or something of the sort, and we'll probably get *that* wrong, too. But it will all come out in the wash, *Puzzled*. You seem to feel that if we had a reformed calendar you'd have to start all over again. It wouldn't be as bad as that, really. It may be upsetting at first, but life itself is upsetting. Once you get that into your head, you won't feel so flustered about any one reform.

March 4

IF YOU ever intend to acquire a pet porcupine, it's advisable to absorb a few simple truths.

Porcupines do not throw their quills into you, as the old story had it. They only leave them in you when they happen to back into you, or when they slap their tails at you. The quills can be removed from your anatomy by any good surgeon, with or without an anesthetic.

Pet porcupines are not without tender feelings of their own. When caught young and properly raised, they often show marked affection for their owners.

You could always move away.

March 5

THERE are people who make rules on how to converse. They tell you to be a good listener. (Go ahead and listen and see what it gets you.)

Listening may do as an ideal. In actual practice I find that you have to keep going if you want to get a word in edgeways. The best talker I know says she regards conversation as a hand-to-hand struggle to say the most words possible in the

least possible amount of elapsed time and the devil take the hindmost. She gets away with it, too.

Doctor Samuel Johnson wasn't bad at that, either. After talking a blue streak for four or five hours, he was wont to remark: "Well, sir, this has been a good evening. We have had good talk. The communication of mind is always of use. Thought flowed freely this evening." He was right, at that.

As for those little things I stick in my ears, it isn't that I'm not interested. I may have some form of auditory hyperesthesia, the doctor says.

52

March 6

GUESS what English poetess was born at Carlton Hall, Durham, on March 6, 1806, and later wrote the following lines:

> *If thou must love me, let it be for nought*
> *Except for love's sake only.*

She also wrote *Hector in the Garden* and *Bertha in the Lane*, although she seldom mentioned them. She married a gentleman who had beautiful whiskers and wrote *Fifine at the Fair*. You give up? All right then, she had a little dog named Flush and she used to live in Wimpole Street. The answer, of course, is Elizabeth Barrett Browning. This may not add much to your store of knowledge, but it's a start.

March 7

I'D RATHER not tell you about the amoeba, but facts are facts. Amoebas not only divide, they also blend. When it's all over there is one amoeba where there were two. Amoebas blend apparently because they enjoy blending for its own sake.

The amoeba often frequents laboratories. You'll find quite a number of amoebas at Yale, Princeton, and Harvard.

There are good amoebas and bad amoebas.

March 8

IF YOU have nothing better to do, you could brush up on the planets any time now, as all five of the naked-eye ones are visible these nights. Venus is acting as evening star in the

West just after sunset and Mars and Jupiter appear before midnight. Mars is that red one in Virgo and Jupiter is in Libra—you may have more trouble with him. By watching a few hours longer you can catch Saturn and Mercury in Aquarius, if you care that much. Of course, the planets don't snap off and on and they don't spell anything, but you can't have everything. I don't know whether there is any life on these planets or not, human or inhuman. If there are people on them they probably *think* they're human, the same as we do.

March 9

FRANZ JOSEPH GALL, founder of phrenology, was born at Tiefenbrunn, near Pforzheim, on March 9, 1758. He said you could tell a person's disposition, character, mental powers, and special talents by feeling the bumps on his head. As this was obviously ridiculous from any point of view, a great many people believed it, until they lost interest and took up something else. Even if there were anything in it, phrenology is too complicated for our modern taste. For instance, the bump of concentrativeness is just below the obelion and over the lambda—well, anyway, the lambda must be under the obelion somewhere. Most of us have the same trouble with the glottis and the epiglottis. We know that the epiglottis is right on top of the glottis, but where is the glottis?

March 10

"DEAR SIR: Do you approve of cantaloupe-scraping?
                                          "Uneasy"

I suppose you mean is it correct to dig, gouge, or otherwise

excavate the last possible morsel of the melon, even if you have to eat part of the rind? My answer would be Yes, and No.

Compulsive cantaloupe-scraping is looked down upon in some quarters. My own feeling is that (a) iced cantaloupe is probably the best food ever invented, and that (b) you're only young once. A good plan is to watch the hostess. She may be one of us.

March 11

"DEAR SIR: I am eighteen years old and much interested in weather conditions. Do you think our winters are growing milder?

"Brown Eyes"

I don't know what to make of young people nowadays. At your age, *Brown Eyes*, you might be better employed than worrying about whether our winters are growing milder. Is this just morbid curiosity, or are you trying to prove that your grandfather is fibbing about all those blizzards he went through in the old days?

Well, our winters were growing milder for a while, but it wouldn't surprise me if they kept getting colder and colder. You just can't count on the weather, *Brown Eyes*. I find it hard to believe that the snow was always up to the second story windows, the way your grandfather thinks it was. By the way, the blizzard of '88 began on March 11. Does that thrill you?

March 12

BISHOP BERKELEY, Irish philosopher and champion of tar-water as a cure for nervous colic, was born in Kilkenny County on March 12, 1685. He achieved fame for some very strange ideas about tables and chairs and other solid objects. Supposing you saw a table, he held that the table was there, all right, and then again it wasn't. He said that since the *being* of tables lies in their being *perceived*, the table was there only because of your idea that it was there, but when you asked him what gave you the idea he would shut up like a clam. This form of reasoning was called British Idealism. It was finally abandoned because it was too wearing in the long run. Bishop Berkeley was said to be excellent company if you could keep him off tables.

His thoughts on tar-water were contained in books entitled *Thoughts on Tar-Water* and *Further Thoughts on Tar-Water*.

March 13

ON MARCH 13, 1930, Doctor V. M. Slipher, director of the Lowell Observatory, announced the discovery of Pluto, the ninth and most distant planet of our solar system, which had been observed several weeks before and held incommunicado by the doctor himself and his associates. For a year or so I had high hopes for Pluto, and what came of them? Pluto is only one-tenth as large as the earth, it is extremely cold, it has no atmosphere, and all it is good for is to pull Uranus and Neptune out of their orbits a little—not enough to matter, just enough to annoy one.

Pluto is about 3,800,000,000 miles from the sun, or forty times as far as we are. That suits me perfectly.

March 14

ON MARCH 14, 1700, William Dampier, English explorer and buccaneer, landed on the coast of Australia and discovered the kangaroo. At least, he discovered some jumping animals which I always took to be kangaroos and which, to the best of my knowledge and belief, *were* kangaroos. I am sorry to find that John Masefield, poet laureate of England, considered these animals as nothing but kangaroo rats, probably because they seem to have been smaller than the kangaroos he himself was used to. Much as I respect Mr. Masefield's work, I can't see the poetry of dragging kangaroo rats into the picture at this late date. Wallabies I might grant him, or wombats, but kangaroo rats—never!

March 15

OF THE Seven Sages of ancient Greece, the one who is most remembered today is Solon, the Law Giver. You seldom hear of the other six Wise Men. They turned out to be not so wise as they had seemed at the time.

Besides legalizing the brothels, Solon performed many other notable deeds. He has been called by some historians "the founder of Athenian democracy." Solon also got off some pithy sayings which helped build his reputation as a wise man.

"Pursue worthy aims" was one. "Shun evil company" was another. It is said that he is the author of the apothegm: "Nothing too much." But the favorite of most Athenians was his "Never tell a lie." That will give you an idea.

March 16

JAMES MADISON, fourth President of the United States, was born at Port Conway, Virginia, on March 16, 1751. As most of us can name only about four Presidents in their proper order, starting with George Washington, Madison generally gets into the list, although he is sometimes nosed out by Monroe on account of the Monroe Doctrine. Native-born Americans also have trouble remembering that John Adams was our second President because it seems as though Thomas Jefferson really should have been. One can always check up on our Presidents by asking some foreigner—they have to know those things before we regard them as equals. President Madison is chiefly remembered as the husband of Dolly Madison, with whom he got along splendidly by letting her do as she pleased. This was called the Madison Doctrine.

March 17

"DEAR SIR: Can hermits cook? I've been worried about this for years, and I hope you can clear it up for me once and for all.

"Gregarious"

We hermits don't cook much ourselves, *Gregarious*. The kindest thing that can be said about my own cooking is that perhaps I am, in a small way, somewhat of an authority on how to open tin cans. That is really the secret of hermit cookery. All hermits worthy of the name are experts, as some one has observed, on new and appetizing ways of opening a can of beans.

One of the reasons is that hermits never think of food until they are hungry—practically starving. Then they eat all at once. They simply haven't the patience to wait until they can cook something that might take five or ten minutes. If there's a can of beans around, it has to take its chances.

March 18

JOHN C. CALHOUN, famous American statesman, was born in South Carolina on March 18, 1782. He was Vice President under John Quincy Adams and also under Andrew Jackson. He was a powerful orator and did all he could to bring on the War of 1812, during which the British captured Washington and burned down the White House. Many amusing anecdotes are told of Calhoun. For instance—well, I was going to say that he once exclaimed: "I would rather be right than President!" but that seems to have been Henry Clay. And I'm afraid it was Daniel Webster who composed his great speeches while fishing. Anyway, Calhoun's handwriting was terrible, or was that Horace Greeley?

March 19

DAVID LIVINGSTONE, Scottish explorer and missionary, was born near Glasgow on March 19, 1813. When quite young he went to Africa and stayed there most of his time, making important discoveries in geography and hydrography

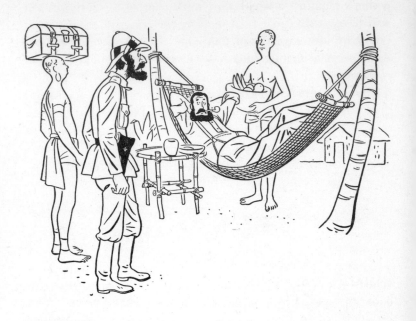

and converting the heathen and living at such places as Mabotsa and Shupanga and Ujiji. That was what he wanted to do, but most people could not understand it. Most people think that if you do not live where *they* do, you are missing a lot. So Henry M. Stanley went to Africa to find Livingstone and bring him back to civilization, and he finally found him at Ujiji and said: "Doctor Livingstone, I presume?" Well, it turned out that Livingstone wasn't lost at all and that he wanted to stay there, which he did. This teaches that your chances of being let alone, even if you go to Ujiji, are pretty slim.

March 20

TOADS can be useful in exterminating ants. If you are bothered by ants, let half a dozen toads loose in the house. In a very short time you will no longer have ants. Of course you *will* have toads.

A man who should know has said: "The toad shows certain excellences of moral or intellectual character."

I don't go that far, but I think they're nice to have around. Better than ants, certainly.

March 21

AMONG things you might be thinking about today is the vernal equinox—it's March 21, you know. The vernal equinox is the point at which the sun apparently crosses the celestial equator toward the north, or you can say it is the moment at which this occurs, or you can simply say: "Hooray! Spring is here!" Exactly why the sun does this on March 21 is a long story. At one time the sun began falling behind until it finally got to crossing the celestial equator on March 11 and everybody was very much upset. The Gregorian Calendar fixed that, and now everything is all right again, unless it's being hushed up. I don't see why spring should not begin on March 11 if it wants to. I'd say the sooner the better. When all's said, spring is probably the least obnoxious of all the four seasons.

March 22

PERSONS born from now until April 21 are under the sign of Aries, the Ram. Aries rules the head and in some instances it does a much better job than in others. Aries persons possess great executive ability and almost always get along, if they have plenty of financial backing and lots of luck. They must guard against a tendency to step on the tips of umbrellas which are dragged along in front of them. Eminent Aries persons include Prince von Bismarck, Leon Gambetta, Oliver Cromwell, William Wadsworth, Harry Houdini, Nicholas Murray Butler, Charlie Chaplin, Henry James, Booker T. Washington, Branch Cabell, Charles Evans Hughes, Mary Pickford, Rosa Bonheur, William Waldorf Astor, Algernon Charles Swinburne, Wilbur Wright, George Arliss, Bud Fisher, Raphael Sanzio, Cy Young, William Shakespeare, and Laura Jean Libbey.

March 23

"DEAR SIR: Must *R.s.v.p.* invitations alway be answered in the third person?

"Anxious"

They really should be, *Anxious*. It may help you to know that my own stock reply to *R.s.v.p.* invitations runs as follows:

"Mr. Cuppy will attend Mr. and Mrs. Titherington van Whoozis's garden party and exhibition of fireworks three weeks from next Saturday night if he feels good and like it at the time, and if he doesn't get some other idea on the way there, but not otherwise. He believes that life is too short and too beautiful to waste even a part of it going places where he would rather be shot than go, and Mr. and Mrs. Titherington van Whoozis have a nerve to expect it. Mr. Cuppy cannot be intimidated by the letters *R.s.v.p.* into mortgaging his future in such a manner as to preclude his use of free choice and judgment in the pursuit of happiness or its equivalent, and whoever thinks he can is barking up the wrong tree."

You would be surprised, *Anxious*, how this simplifies my social life.

March 24

IF YOU overslept today, don't feel guilty. You might try meditating on the dormouse, a cousin of the house mouse.

Dormice are always sleepy. They know little or nothing of what goes on in the world, as they sleep for six months each year and about half the time during the remaining six months. Thus, they are conscious only a fourth of the time and miss a lot of foolishness.

Dormice are prettier than house mice. Why wouldn't they be, with all that sleep?

March 25

MAYBE you hadn't noticed, but Mother Nature is getting into her stride again. Rhubarb is up, the two-spined stickle-backs are courting in the creeks, and the downy woodpeckers are drilling holes in the dawn. The downy woodpecker may be distinguished from the other four hundred kinds of wood-peckers by its peculiar note. Mr. F. Schuyler Mathews, a veteran authority, states that the downy woodpecker utters a metallic *chink chink*. Mr. Aretas A. Saunders, another veteran authority, swears that it goes *keep* or *kawick kawick* and in extreme cases *he he he he he he he he he he he he he hi hi ha ha ho*. I haven't made up my mind yet how it goes. Many people have lived fine and useful lives without going into the question at all.

March 26

ONE of my favorite great sayings of history is the crack Talleyrand got off: "He who was not living before 1789 knows nothing of the charms of living."

But for a good all-around famous saying that will stand the test of time, I suggest the remark attributed to Valdemar IV, King of Denmark: "Tomorrow will be another day."

There *is* a rumor that Valdemar IV may have heard Valdemar III say this, but I don't put any stock in it. Maybe it isn't the brightest statement you ever heard, but the king was probably hard up for conversation. Anyway, it's better than "It's a small world, after all."

How good does a saying have to be to become a famous saying? Murad III, Sultan of Turkey in 1574, made the grade with this priceless *mot*: "I am hungry; bring me something to eat." I could have said that myself.

March 27

ON MARCH 27, 1513, Juan Ponce de León discovered Florida, where he believed there was a Fountain of Youth

that would make him eighteen again instead of fifty-three. He drank from every spring in sight and was much disappointed to find that he still had some gray hair and a crick in his back. Nowadays we know that a man is as old as he feels, and that's the catch in the whole thing. Ponce de León is sometimes looked upon as an awful old grumbler for wanting to find the Fountain of Youth. Well, anyway, he wasn't kidding himself.

March 28

"DEAR SIR: What ten books would you take to a desert island?

"Alumna"

Wouldn't you rather hear about the trouble the Australians had with St. John's-wort, a wild flower that has become a pest in those parts? Believing it to be British St. John's-wort, the Australians imported some British insects to destroy it, but it turned out to be a continental species and the insects wouldn't touch it. So there were the Australians with a lot of strange insects in addition to the usual dingoes, echidnas, and duck-billed platypuses, and I haven't been able to learn what happened next. I'm not going to a desert island, *Alumna*. I'm staying right here by the telegraph wires.

March 29

JOHN TYLER, tenth President of the United States, was born at Greenway, Virginia, on March 29, 1790. He was elected Vice President on the Whig ticket in 1840 and moved up a notch when President William Henry Harrison died a month after his inauguration. Tyler spent the rest of the term quarreling with the Whigs, who had decided they didn't like him after all, so he had very little fun during office hours. He was married twice and had fourteen children. Harrison and Tyler won the election with the slogan, "Tippecanoe and Tyler, too," invented by a Mr. Orson E. Woodbury. I suppose people knew what that meant in 1840, but nowadays it's a lost art. And guess who was our *next* President. James K. Polk!

March 30

ON THIS date in 1930 the skull of the Peking Man was examined by scientists at a meeting of the Geological Society of China, in Peking, and pronounced awfully backward. In Menominee, Michigan, a sheriff broke into a padlocked saloon to rescue a starving cat, and in Owsley Fork, Kentucky, a deputy sheriff shot and killed a farmer who had a gallon of whisky in his home. At the naval arms conference in London, there was an international discussion based upon the first paragraph of Article XVI of the League of Nations covenant, which provided that any nation which goes to war without keeping all its obligations under Articles XII, XIII, and XIV of said Covenant shall be considered *ipso facto* to have gone to war. Yet some people say there's no progress.

March 31

"DEAR SIR: Do you know any way to cure a husband of constant punning? I am almost at the end of my strength.
"Anonymous"

66

I know how to cure him, *Anonymous*, but it may not come to that if you follow my directions. When your husband makes a pun just ignore it. Every time you say, "Oh, darling, *please* stop that, it's driving me mad!" you merely aggravate the case. He thinks you're urging him on to further achievement of the same sort and he will go to great lengths to oblige you. I'm sure he would stop if he knew your real opinion of puns. As an habitual punster, however, he is constitutionally unfitted to know any number of things. Of course, a policy of sepulchral silence on your part may eventually do things to your love. It may not even improve your husband's condition. I'm afraid you brought this on yourself, *Anonymous*.

APRIL

April 1

ANTIQUARIANS can't decide who started the custom of
April fooling, or hunting the gowk, as it is called in Scotland.
It seems likely, however, that the Java Man (*Pithecanthropus
erectus*) had already begun to stretch strings across the side-
walk where old Java Ladies would trip over them and break
their hips. An examination of the Java Man's skull convinces
me that he fell out of an apple tree at an early age, landing
spang on the head, so naturally he *would* do those things.
April 1 provides an outlet for practical jokers at just the
right time—it's a little too early for rocking the boat and a little
too late for shooting the neighbors by mistake while out hunting ducks.

71

April 2

ON APRIL 2, 1702, there passed away a humbly born and quite untutored French admiral named Jean Bart, who did a lot for Louis XIV in the way of scuttling Dutch and English ships. When Louis so far unbent as to grant him an audience and high office in person, the brave Jean rather surprised him by saying: "Sire, you have done well in this!" And when the king graciously remarked: "Jean Bart, I would I had ten thousand men like thee!" the simple seaman replied, somewhat to the amusement of the courtiers: "I can well believe it, Your Majesty!"

Personally, I like Jean's simple statements of fact much better than Louis's own *L'État, c'est moi!* I don't care for the sentiment expressed in *The State, it is me!* not to mention the grammar.

April 3

JOHN BURROUGHS, beloved American naturalist, was born near Roxbury, New York, on April 3, 1837. I can't find the reference this minute, but didn't he once say that he considered the crowing of the barnyard cock the most beautiful sound in nature? Or was it Henry Thoreau? To tell you the truth, I wouldn't put it past both of them. Burroughs and Thoreau were fine old fellows. They loved the birds and the flowers, and they wrote very well, but I often wonder if something wasn't wrong with their ears. If the crowing of cocks sounded the same to them as it does to me, they *couldn't* have liked it. From what I have been able to learn of the human race most of them don't care one way or the other about the

crowing of roosters. They don't seem to notice it, even. Amazing, the human race.

April 4

YOU may not realize that this is the birthday of Grinling Gibbons, celebrated interior decorator, who was born April 4, 1648, either in London or in Rotterdam. His specialty was carving pendants, swags, and garlands of flowers, fruit, foliage, grain, and game on paneled walls in the reigns of Charles II,

James II, William and Mary, Anne, and George I. Grinling Gibbons' wooden oranges are probably the best wooden oranges ever carved, and his wooden aspidistras have never been surpassed. Grinling Gibbons' career may strike you as a little strange until you get the idea that wooden oranges have their place in the universal scheme—then everything will be perfectly clear.

April 5

GUESS who wrote the following lines:

*As sea-foam blown of the winds, as blossoms of brine
    that is drifted
Hither and yon on the barren breast of the breeze,
Though we wander on gusts of a god's breath, shaken and
    shifted,
The salt of us stings and is sore for the sobbing seas.*

No, it wasn't Swinburne. It was H. C. Bunner, showing how Swinburne might have written the first few lines of *Home, Sweet Home.* And now that the subject has come up, Algernon Charles Swinburne was born in London on April 5, 1837. He had a wild time and wrote wonderful poems until 1880, when a Mr. Theodore Watts-Dunton reformed him and took him to Putney, where he lived a blameless life for the next thirty years and wrote a lot of poems that weren't so hot. So far as I know, nobody has ever written much immortal poetry while living a blameless life at Putney. It may be just a coincidence.

April 6

"DEAR SIR: Where do you stand on the 100,000,000-year-old ophiacadon's egg discovered a while back in central Texas?

"Housewife"

Generally speaking, I'm against it. If this egg is really 100,-000,000 years old, that would make it older than the dinosaur eggs found by Roy Chapman Andrews in the Gobi Desert and therefore one of the oldest fossil eggs known to man, but that doesn't matter to me. In order to appeal to me, *Housewife*, an egg has to have more than mere age. There is such a thing as sentiment. Some of us feel a real affection for Mr. Andrews's dinosaur eggs, and I, for one, am not going to switch to ophiacadon's eggs all of a sudden. I'm fond of dinosaurs, too. They had only a spoonful of brains each, but why worry? With a dinosaur at least you know where you are.

April 7

SOME people grow up with a deep attachment for the family sponge. They would rush into a burning building to rescue it, and they wouldn't think of moving without it.

Well, a sponge can be useful as a repository for germs. There are 2,500 kinds of sponges. All of them consist largely of holes.

Sponges have no nervous systems. They live mainly in warm waters—the Mediterranean, the West Indies, and places like that. They reproduce by means of gemmules, whatever they are. Your guess is as good as mine.

75

April 8

LORENZO DE' MEDICI, alias Lorenzo the Magnificent, the great Florentine banker and patron of Renaissance art and letters, passed away on April 8, 1492. Which reminds me that literary patronage seems to be on the decline, or maybe I meet the wrong people. I once asked the only millionaire I ever met if he wouldn't like to support some struggling author who had lots of talent but couldn't seem to get along, somehow. I didn't succeed in getting his views, because he pulled out his watch and said he had just remembered a very important engagement. Nothing much came of *that* conversation.

April 9

"DEAR SIR: To settle a bet, please tell me whether Sir Francis Bacon wrote Shakespeare's plays. Answer yes or no.
"Bewildered"

About all I care to say at present is that Francis Bacon, Baron Verulam and Viscount St. Albans, wrote some fine essays, became Lord Chancellor of England, was convicted of bribery and corruption, and died on April 9, 1626, of bronchitis contracted while stuffing a fowl with snow. Some very charming and lovable people believe that he wrote Shakespeare's plays. You can't spot these people at sight. Only an expert can tell that there is anything—uh—unusual about them—that is, in their lucid intervals. This department does not answer bets, but maybe you can read between the lines.

April 10

BUTTON GWINNETT, one of the fifty-six signers of the Declaration of Independence, was baptized in the city of Gloucester, Gloucestershire, England, on April 10, 1735— and maybe I didn't have a time finding *that* out. He was named Button after his mother's cousin, Miss Barbara Button, of the Glamorganshire Buttons. He came to the United States about 1765, settled in Georgia, and seems to have devoted himself largely to not signing anything but the Declaration of Independence. As his signatures are extremely rare and valuable, I sent the following note to a list of deserving friends last Christmas: "Merry Christmas and Happy New Year, and here is a signature of Button Gwinnett.—*Button Gwinnett*." The joke didn't go over too well. Most of my friends had never heard of Button Gwinnett.

April 11

"DEAR SIR: What do the English mean by the expression, 'Cholmondeley weighs fourteen stone'?
                                                        "Bothered"

They mean that Cholmondeley weighs fourteen times fourteen pounds, or 196 pounds—a stone equalling fourteen pounds avoirdupois in their language when applied to Englishmen or other large animals—otherwise, a stone equals anywhere from eight to twenty-four pounds. Apparently they do not wish to say right out that Cholmondeley weighs 196 pounds, and in my opinion they don't even know it. Since the human brain is not so constituted as to be able to multiply fourteens at will there is always a large margin of uncertainty

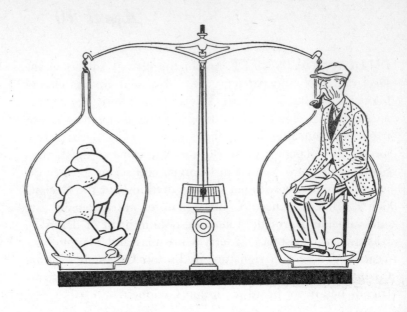

about people's weights in England. They get some sort of general impression, however, and that seems to satisfy them.

April 12

HENRY CLAY, one of our greatest Americans, was born in Hanover County, Virginia, on April 12, 1777. Cross out statements which you know to be untrue: (1) Henry Clay was the eleventh President of the United States. (2) Henry Clay was a fine orator. (3) He once said: "I propose to fight it out on this line if it takes all Summer." (4) He was called the Great Pacificator because he believed in Free Silver. (5) He discovered electricity by flying a kite.

Well, anyway, he *did* say: "I would rather be right than President." It may sound like sour grapes, but I would rather be practically anything than President.

April 13

"DEAR SIR: Please tell me some thrilling way to cook navy beans.

"Urgent"

Boil them till done but not mashed. Take a bit of butter the size of a walnut, half an onion chopped fine. Do them together in a frying pan till the onion is done. Dash in a little flour and soup enough to make a gravy. Put in your beans, let them boil, and season with pepper and salt. If you don't like the result, blame Thomas Jefferson, who wrote this recipe with his own hand and inserted it into his family cook book. I don't understand about the soup, but you may. Yes, this is Thomas Jefferson's birthday—born April 13, 1743, in Shadwell, Albemarle County, Virginia.

April 14

IF YOU want to study the Bomdidae, or bumblebees, there's ..o law against it. All you need is lots of enthusiasm, some powers of observation, and a good supply of ammonia, vinegar, or soda.

There are many quaint superstitions about bees. The natives of Suffolk believe that if a marriage occurs in your family you must go and tell the bees about it or they will become fretful. The custom of telling the bees about your personal affairs is known as "telling it to the bees." In other quarters it is said to be unlucky to have a stray swarm of bees settle on or in your dwelling. I should think so.

April 15

THIS is the birthday of John Law, Scotch financial genius, who was born in Edinburgh on April 15, 1671. As a youth he studied political economy until he had developed a system, and later he wrote a book called *Money and Trade Considered, with a Proposal for Supplying the Nation with Money.* He then went to France and invented the Mississippi Scheme, by means of which the French government and people were all to become very rich in no time. The Mississippi Scheme was practically certain to work, but somehow the shareholders kept getting sorer and sorer and poor Mr. Law had to run for it. Mr. Law knew more about political economy than any man of his time, but that is what happened just the same. Now that I think it over, maybe there *is* no way of making a lot of money.

April 16

ON THIS date in 1904 a great and good man passed away—Sir Samuel Smiles, author of *Character, Thrift, Duty, with Illustrations of Courage, Patience, and Endurance* and *Self-Help, with Illustrations of Character, Conduct, and Perseverance.* Sir Samuel believed that a lifetime of spotless virtue and grim, unrelenting toil would get you somewhere in the end, and I shouldn't be a bit surprised if he was right. I'm not entirely sure, because Sir Samuel wrote about all the things that I never quite got around to.

April 17

IN ADDITION to other forms of nonsense, Aristotle is credited with promoting the syllogism, if not actually inventing it.

That's the line of reasoning that goes like this:

> Socrates is rational;
> Socrates is a man;
> Therefore, man is rational.

Even at the time, everybody knew perfectly well that Socrates was not rational. Subsequently an unsung Great Thinker has pointed out that "the major premise of the syllogism takes for granted precisely the point to be proved."

These days syllogisms have given way to Twenty Questions and Charades. All to the good, I'd say.

April 18

'TWAS April 18, 1775, that Paul Revere made his famous ride from somewhere or other to Lexington, I think it was,

shouting "The British are coming!" at every house on the way. We all know the story perfectly well, yet one or two historians have cast doubt upon it because Paul's private accounts contain nothing to indicate that he ever owned a horse. All right, gentlemen, *my* private accounts contain nothing about a horse, either, but I certainly owned one—that is, a pony. His name was Blacky. I merely mention it in case it should ever come up.

April 19

"DEAR SIR: Well, I suppose you're all set to tell us some stale anecdote about Benjamin Disraeli, Earl of Beaconsfield, who passed away on April 19, 1881. Am I right?
"Junior"

No, *Junior,* for once you are wrong. If I *were* going to pester you with a Disraeli anecdote, however, I might possibly dig up that thing his wife used to say to him: "Oh, yes, I know you married me for my money, but if you were to marry me again you'd marry me for love, wouldn't you?" To which Dizzy invariably answered: "Yes, of course I would."

I've always thought that was kind of cute of her—and of him, too, for that matter. You may notice, *Junior,* that this anecdote is about *Lady* Beaconsfield. It isn't so awfully funny, but you brought it on yourself.

April 20

MARCUS AURELIUS ANTONINUS, Roman Emperor and Stoic philosopher, was born in Rome on April 20 in the year A.D. 121—or, as some state, on April 6, 21, or 26. He is famous for his remarkable virtue, which, so far as I can learn, he never denied. At the age of twelve he went around telling grown-ups how to behave, and later he wrote his *Meditations*, teaching that we should all cultivate wisdom, justice, fortitude, temperance, duty, frugality, resignation, self-control, and miscellaneous. Nobody has anything much on Marcus Aurelius except that he was a little too fond of torturing people who didn't agree with him. Personally, I don't believe that nasty story about the time he—well, why rake that up? I always say you should never repeat back-fence gossip unless you practically saw it with your own eyes.

April 21

THE vicuña makes a nice household pet, if you live 10,000 feet up. Vicuñas have soft, silky hair and run wild in the Andes.

Most male vicuñas travel around with their own private flock of six to fifteen loyal and affectionate females. When the male is killed or wounded by a hunter, the females gather round, sniffling and carrying on. Then *they* can be shot, too.

When a female is shot, the male issues a warning cry, and the flock takes off at high speed. The wounded female is left behind, to ponder on such subjects as chivalry, gratitude, and gallantry.

April 22

ALL babies born from now until May 22 will be under the Sign of Taurus, the Bull, and this may make quite a difference. Famous persons who started out as Taurus babies include Doctor Albert Einstein, Bing Crosby, Sir James Matthew Barrie, Dolly Madison, Niccolò Machiavelli, Alfred Krupp, Florence Nightingale, Cyrus H. McCormick, Lionel Barrymore, Maria Theresa, Herbert Spencer, Wilbur Wright, Honorable Stephen A. Douglas, Dante Gabriel Rossetti, Johannes Brahms, Irving Berlin, John James Audubon, Adolf Hitler, Saint Vincent de Paul, Doctor Sigmund Freud, Maximilien François Marie Isidore de Robespierre, and Shirley Temple. Supposing *you* tell us what kind of babies are born under Taurus.

April 23

SPEAKING of Shakespeare, and darned if this isn't his birthday, one of the least acute of his critics was King George III of England, who once said to Fanny Burney: "Was there ever such stuff as a great part of Shakespeare? Only one must not say so! But what think you? What? Is there not sad stuff? What? What?" And when shown some of Blake's drawings he cried: "What? What? What? Take them away—take them away!"

George III had the happy faculty of spotting a first-rate performance the instant it reared its ugly head and hating it like poison. Even today you'll find people like that, and for the same reason.

April 24

FIRST there was the mastodon, then came the mammoth, and now we have the elephant we know today. Does that clear things up any?

The mastodon's teeth were too weak. He probably didn't get enough roughage and his gums must have grown tender.

The mastodon was a second or third cousin of the mammoth, which lived during the Ice Age in Europe, Asia, and North America. If you have seen an elephant, you have practically seen a mammoth. He averaged only nine or ten feet in height but he was considered pretty big. He died off after a while, perhaps because he needed too much food and heat in an Ice Age.

In the Pleistocene Era, there were more than twenty kinds of elephants. Now there are only two. That's plenty.

April 25

SOMETIMES I get a little tired of having people tell me that I'm nervous. They probably mean that I cannot write articles in a room full of wild Indians and that I have a tendency to jump when somebody sneaks up behind me and yells "Boo!" I try to concentrate on the fact that in some definitions the word *nervous* is not an opprobrious epithet at all. The first definition of *nervous* in my dictionary runs: "Possessing nerve; sinewy; strong; vigorous; forcible; spirited." And here's the second: "Hence, possessing or manifesting vigor of mind; characterized by strength in sentiment or style; as, a *nervous* writer." Very well, then, I'm a nervous writer.

April 26

DAVID HUME, Scottish philosopher and historian, was born in Edinburgh on April 26, 1711. He suffered from hypochondria in youth and shortly thereafter wrote his *Treatise of Human Nature,* in which he completely explained human nature to his own satisfaction. Hume was a great believer in reason and said that we should follow it at all times. This sounds much brighter than it really is, because it can't be done in the first place—it's surprising what great thinkers will overlook when they get going. Hume's dear old mother once remarked: "Our Davie is a fine, good-natured creature, but uncommon weak-minded."

April 27

"DEAR SIR: How did President Ulysses Simpson Grant get such a name, anyway?

"Anxious"

Well, it's quite a story. At first he was named Hiram Ulysses Grant—Hiram on general principles and Ulysses because it seemed like a good idea at the time. Then the family sort of dropped the Hiram and called him Ulysses and the neighbors called him Useless. Congressman Thomas L. Hamer, who knew the lad simply as Ulysses, got him registered at West Point as Ulysses Simpson Grant, doubtless on the theory that if he had a middle name it would probably be Simpson. So the boys dropped the Ulysses and called him Sam. It turned out all right because General H. U. Grant would sound terrible. He was born at Point Pleasant, Ohio, on April 27, 1822.

April 28

DID I ever tell you about my barometer? It certainly made all the difference.

One thing I found out by reading it—just noticing where the needle or pointer is won't do you any good unless you know whether the thing is rising or falling. That is, whether it's going to the right or the left of the other needle—the one my cleaning woman keeps twirling when I'm not looking. A rapid rise indicates unsettled weather and a rapid fall, say, from continued cool to cloudy and warmer indicates that Louella has called.

Besides, you must take the wind into consideration. A rise with balmy southerly winds means fine weather, as you would probably know for yourself without consulting a barometer. A fall in winter with dry air and increasing chill means it may snow. I'll say this for the barometer—it uses plenty of good common sense.

April 29

"DEAR SIR: I am completely fed up with April showers. What can I do about it?

"*Soaked*"

It's too late to do anything this year, as April is almost over. I can only suggest that parts of the coast of Peru, certain areas in northern Chile, and much of western China are practically free from April showers. Then there's the Lop Desert, just north of Tibet, where it hasn't rained to speak of for two thousand years and where nobody tells you that rain is good for the crops. You sound awfully young to me, *Soaked*. Haven't you ever heard that there's always something?

April 30

SIR John Lubbock, English naturalist and person of affairs, was born in London on April 30, 1834. He was a big banker and politician, but he is chiefly known as the man who had a tame wasp. He caught his wasp young, fed her on his hand, stroked her on the back, and carried her in a bottle on his journeys, and she only stung him once when she was flustered by a train conductor. She is now in the British Museum with many other odd things. Sir John's scientific works aroused great interest, but his idea of having a tame wasp around never got very far—it just didn't catch on, somehow.

MAY

May 1

I'M ALWAYS glad to see May 1 arrive, though I don't make much of a fuss about it. I don't go a-Maying to bring home the first gay blossoms of the greater stitchwort. I don't even care much for the greater stitchwort. Nor is it the return of the birds that fills me with an inner peace—I haven't even missed them.

No, I'm afraid it's just some subterranean stirring of my instinct of self-preservation that gives me such a kick every May Day. I feel that anyhow I've got through the winter. By and large, that's quite a feeling.

May 2

"DEAR SIR: Please outline the main facts in the history of the umbrella.

"Old Grad"

I'm really not up to it today, *Old Grad*. Umbrellas, however, are believed to be of great antiquity, as they are represented in the pictures of some extremely old and ugly Assyrians—the uglier the Assyrian the surer he was to own an umbrella. In my opinion, there have always been certain people who know a little more than they should and therefore carry umbrellas at exactly the right time and place, if they have to start twenty-four hours before the first drop falls.

I won't say that I dislike these people, but I will say that their horrible rightness, nine times out of ten, is not a very lovable quality. There's one fact for you, anyway.

May 3

NICCOLÒ MACHIAVELLI, Italian statesman and author, was born at Florence on May 3, 1469. He is famous for writing *Il Principe* or *The Prince*, in which he showed how to run a government without bothering about high ideals and such things. Machiavelli believed that politics was a sort of game to be won by the smartest player and he would even try to mislead his opponents in order to get the better of them.

This was very wrong of him, because we should always use perfect candor in every relation of life and tell all we know to Tom, Dick, and Harry—at least, so I've been told.

Sometimes one really does meet people who say whatever they think, right to your face. So you know how it works.

May 4

HOORAY for Thomas Henry Huxley, English biologist, who was born at Ealing on May 4, 1825. He had only two years of schooling and soon became about the brightest man in England, excepting maybe Darwin.

Professor Huxley tried to make us think scientifically and not just hit-or-miss, and you can see the results of his campaign even today.

It is not generally known that he delivered a lecture on herrings at the International Fishery Exhibition at Norwich in 1881, when he gave a rough estimate of the number of herrings then in existence. I forget his figures now, but they were probably too small.

May 5

THE herring has been called the poor man's fish, though it has been relished by royalty. Charles V, Emperor of the Holy Roman Empire, once made a journey with the Queen of Hungary to the tomb of William Benkelen, or Benckels, of Biervlet, near Sluys, who invented the pickled herring in 1416. And was that a red-letter day for the herring!

Charles V and the Queen of Hungary both loved pickled herrings, but Charles would hardly have gone to Biervlet if the Queen hadn't insisted upon it. She was either his sister or his aunt, I forget which, and she was one of those old ladies who always get their way. She was forever bossing Charles around, and he was supposed to be the most powerful monarch on earth. He should have put his foot down.

The Hanseatic League, of course, owed much of its strength to the herring fisheries of the Baltic. It lost out when the herrings suddenly left the Baltic and went to the North Sea. Some say the herrings left the Baltic because of the noise at

the Battle of Copenhagen, but I can't seem to find any Battle
of Copenhagen that jibes with the Hanseatic League or anywhere near it.

Before I decide the point I want to brush up on who belonged to the Hanseatic League and what it was for. Meanwhile, your guess is as good as mine.

May 6

ABOUT this time of year we should all brush up on Vega.
It's one of *the* things to do in May.

Vega is in the constellation Lyra and is the fourth bright-esL star in the heavens, and you'll find it rising in the north-eastern sky around 8 P.M., with luck. Vega shines with a bright bluish light and never does anything unusual, like that Nova Herculis that got into the papers a while back—it doesn't have to because it's a first magnitude star anyhow.

Our solar system is moving toward Vega at the rate of twelve miles a second, and in my opinion we'll never get there. I can't prove it, but those things simply don't happen.

May 7

"DEAR SIR: Who was it made that crack about Robert Browning's poetry and what else do you know?
"Fan"

You probably mean Douglas Jerrold, who started to read *Sordello* while convalescing after a severe illness, turned deadly pale, and exclaimed: "My God! I'm an idiot. My health is restored, but my mind's gone. I can't understand two consecutive lines of an English poem."

The truth was that neither Mr. Jerrold nor Mr. Browning had gone completely cuckoo—it was about fifty-fifty. And that reminds me—Robert Browning was born in Camberwell, London, on May 7, 1812.

May 8

THERE are people almost anywhere you go. There are people who save old paper bags and pieces of string. They never do anything with them, so far as I can see. There are people who like pineapple pie and men who carry canes. There are people who want you to come and look at the sunset. When you say you hate sunsets, they won't believe you. There are people who will rush up and tell you what you just got through telling *them*. What's the idea?

There are people who go to bed at exactly the same time every night. There are people who love to hear crickets chirp —it sounds so cozy.

There are married couples who never had a cross word and maybe that's what's wrong with them. There are people who think the whale is a fish. They may have something there.

There are old gentlemen who spend ten minutes on sniffing all the cigars in the place while you're trying to buy a pack of cigarettes and go on with your life. There are people who play the piano. They go around renting apartments in buildings inhabited by nervous wrecks. They seem to pick out these buildings by instinct.

There are people who get on your nerves. There are old grouches.

P.S.—And there are some very wonderful people. There must be.

May 9

SPEAKING of current crime, and how people used to have *some* respect for law and order, 'twas on May 9, 1671, that Colonel Thomas Blood and a couple of pals stole the crown of England and a few other parts of the royal regalia out of the Tower of London right in broad daylight. A Captain Beckman chased the thieves and finally recovered everything

except a few jewels that fell out of the crown and got lost in the scuffle.

King Charles II thought it was such a good joke that he pardoned Colonel Blood, who stayed around the court and made a lot of money by bribery and corruption, and the moral of this little tale is not so good.

May 10

BET you can't guess who was born in Württemberg, Germany, on May 10, 1854—well, it was Ottmar Mergenthaler. He soon got tired of living in Germany and came to the United States, and by 1885 he had invented the linotype.

The linotype casts type in the following manner: When a letter on the keyboard is struck, a matrix (mould) of that letter drops from the magazine to the assembling elevator and goes on that way until the article is finished—I never could get the hang of it myself.

The linotype machine almost thinks, so it is a very good thing to have in a newspaper office.

May 11

THE Tasmanian Devil is so awful that he is protected by the government. He is a ferocious, ungainly-looking marsupial, about the size of a large cat, with a good-sized head, powerful jaws, and a brain not much larger than that of a rabbit. If his brain were larger, think how much meaner he could be.

The mating season is March and April, and the young are usually born in May. They are good tree-climbers.

To express themselves they emit a whining growl, followed by a snarling cough. This unnerved a number of Tasmanians after a while, and the devil was driven from the more settled districts.

The Tasmanian Devil is now found only in Tasmania. If it's all right with the Tasmanians, that's fine with me.

May 12

SPEAKING of cuckoos, you know it's only the European kind that lays its eggs in other birds' nests—at least that was always the story. Well, it turns out that American cuckoos aren't perfect, either, just as I had sort of suspected. Even American bird professors are beginning to admit that our own black-billed and yellow-billed cuckoos sometimes steal other birds' nests, and we can be pretty sure they are holding back worse things, the general nature of which you can probably guess without any broad hints from me. I could have told them that a cuckoo is a cuckoo the world over. I never knew it to fail.

Maybe the time has come for a little plain speaking about the robin, too. Our native robins haven't been helping their reputation for sagacity much lately by building nests on steam cranes in action, flying against windows for days at a time, and otherwise breaking into the newspapers in the wrong way. It develops that a pair of robins started twenty-six nests inside a factory at Willoughby, Ohio, before they could make up their minds. It wouldn't be fair to draw any final conclusions from all this, but one can't help wondering whether robins are as bright as they used to be. Or were they always like that, only we didn't notice it? Or what?

May 13

"DEAR SIR: Please write an article on the jimson weed, and how are you?
"Nature Lover"

I'm about the same, thanks. The Jamestown weed, jimson weed, datura stramonium, thorn apple, devil's trumpet, or stinkwort belongs to the nightshade family and is poisonous to eat, as some of the early Jamestown settlers discovered.

Its flower is white with a tubular calyx, a funnel-form corolla, and a two-lobed stigma, and its fruit is a hard, spiny ovate capsule. You would think the jimson weed was about the last thing anybody would eat, but some people have nothing better to do. By the way, Captain John Smith and his pals arrived at Jamestown on May 13, 1607.

May 14

WHERE would we be today if Gabriel D. Fahrenheit hadn't been born in Danzig on May 14, 1686? Gabriel D. Fahrenheit is the man who thought up the thermometric scale associated with his name, and a very good scale it is, too, although some people use the centigrade scale just to make life more complicated.

He also invented an improved form of hygrometer, an instrument for measuring the humidity. How he ever got interested in such gadgets is unknown to me. There are people who just naturally take to those things.

May 15

CLEMENS Wenzel Nepomuk Lothar Metternich-Winneburg (Prince Metternich to you) was born in Coblenz on May 15, 1773. He became Austria's most famous statesman and practically ran Europe for thirty or forty years.

Metternich was quite a stand-patter and he was finally put out of business by the young radicals of 1848, who were going to fix things in a jiffy. "Well," exclaimed the old diplomat, "I'm sure I don't know what we are coming to when a lot of young whipper-snappers think they can take over *my* job!" I don't know whether he said those very words, but that's the way *I* would have felt about it.

May 16

"DEAR SIR: Would you advise me to add a tessellated darter to my aquarium?

"Fish Lover"

By all means, if you have cool running water (not over sixty degrees) in your aquarium and are not subject to nervous prostration. Tessellated darters are supposed to be colored like the bottoms of the streams they inhabit in the Eastern and Middle Western states, so they remain quiescent much of the time, under the impression that they are invisible, which they aren't especially.

When startled, they dart jerkily hither and thither, as if this would help matters. They also keep turning their heads from side to side in a way that some people find unendurable in a fish. But you may like that.

May 17

DOCTOR Edward Jenner, discoverer of vaccination against smallpox, was born in Gloucestershire, England, on May 17, 1749. In 1796 he inoculated a boy named James Phipps with cowpox from the arm of Miss Sarah Nelmes, who had caught it from a cow named Bossy.

Two months later, when James was inoculated with real smallpox, he didn't get it. A certain Doctor Smyth said that Doctor Jenner was a fiend in human form for scratching James with cowpox and smallpox, but he was no such thing. He was a mild-mannered man with blue eyes, fond of raising roses, taming birds, playing the flute, and writing so-so verses.

May 18

IF YOU saved a nickel every day for a year, at the end of that period you would have 365 nickels, or 366 in Leap Year. It sounds quite wonderful until you think it out. The catch is that you might have been spending the nickels all that time.

Supposing you are a strong character, however, and have succeeded in saving 365 nickels. You have $18.25. Your next move is to put it out at compound interest, as you would be quite capable of doing if you could save nickels in the first place.

You'd be amazed how compound interest counts up, especially when it's compounded every three months. At the end of their first year of work at 2½ per cent compound interest —that is, two years after you saved the first one—your nickels will have earned you the neat little sum of $0.46. (I really thought the figures would be more impressive, or I wouldn't have started this.)

The smartest plan is to begin saving your nickels when you're a child. I understand that a nickel at 4 per cent compound interest, if you can find somebody who'll give you 4 per cent, will just about double itself in forty-five years. Or better yet, have somebody deposit a whopping big sum that you can get at the minute you come of age.

May 19

"DEAR SIR: What is all this talk about putting butter on a cat's paws and why do they do it?

"Admirer"

Some people believe that putting butter on a cat's paws will keep it from running away from home. Mr. Percy Addle-

shaw (*Notes and Queries,* September 25, 1915) inclines to
this view and Mr. C. A. Arkle (same publication, same date)
says there's not much in it.

None of my friends seem to butter their cats, but that
proves nothing, because I would not be likely to know any
cat-butterers, at least after I had found it out. If you want to
get to the bottom of this matter, *Admirer,* I advise you to butter your cat's paws and watch developments. But don't tell
me what happens—I don't care.

May 20

ONCE there was a little Quaker girl named Dorothea Payne,
or Dolly for short, down in Hanover County, Virginia. She
grew up and married John Todd, who soon died, and then
she married a little man named James Madison, who later became President of the United States.

As our First Lady she was famous for her tact, and in my opinion she never displayed this quality to better advantage than when she put completely at his ease a young man who was so excited at meeting her that he tried to cram a teacup into his pocket. Nobody seems to know what happened to the young man afterwards, but I fear the worst. You guessed it —this is Dolly Madison's birthday. She was born May 20, 1768.

May 21

FRANZ VON SUPPÉ, composer of *Dichte und Bauer*, or *Poet and Peasant*, the overture to which is a household word, passed away on this date in 1895. His best known piece is still going strong. It has been arranged and published for fifty-nine different combinations of instruments and has been played by several thousand other combinations, including the piano and comb, as used by two of my little nieces, and the accordion and what-is-it act performed by persons unknown about half a block from my residence every late afternoon, rain or shine.

I often wonder whether other people have heard *Poet and Peasant* as often as I have. If so, why couldn't we all get together and do something about it?

May 22

THIS is the birthday of Richard Wagner, the greatest composer who ever lived, bar none—and I'm glad I've got *that* off my chest. There is a feeling in certain quarters that Bach and Beethoven were greater and that those who prefer them have more beautiful natures than we Wagner fans have. Well, I think I have the lowdown on that aspect of the problem—I happen to *know* some of these people who prefer Bach and Beethoven.

As I was saying, Richard Wagner was born in Leipzig, on May 22, 1813. Bach and Beethoven, indeed!

May 23

GENERAL Ambrose Everett Burnside, who fought on the Union side in the Civil War, was born in Liberty, Indiana, on May 23, 1824. He has been blamed for losing a couple of battles and for wearing an odd kind of whiskers called burnsides or sideburns, a hirsute drapery covering both cheeks and the upper lip and leaving the chin and laryngeal region bare naked—some people say you can have sideburns without a mustache, but that is merely a quibble.

There were whiskers like that before, but somehow they became associated with General Burnside and he never heard the last of them. Practically all the generals in the Civil War had beards or facial foliage of some kind, and most of them just let nature take its course, like Grant and Lee. General Burnside was about the only one who went in for formal landscape gardening. And that reminds me that in his twenties he was getting married to a girl from Kentucky, and when the clergyman asked her if she would have Ambrose for her wedded husband she said no, she wouldn't. I often wonder whether he had the sideburns at the time.

P.S.—The girl finally married another fellow, who told her he'd shoot her if she pulled that on *him*. Young Ambrose got a wife, too, so everything ended happily.

May 24

THEY do say that all babies born from now on until about June 22 will be under the sign of Gemini, or the Twins. The constellation Gemini is ruled by the planet Mercury, whatever that means, so Gemini people are likely to be a little trying at times, unless they watch themselves—they fly off the handle when crossed, especially in childhood. Most Gemini ladies possess much charm and beauty. The men are often flirtatious in youth. They settle down later into useful citizens, and sometimes they wonder what it gets them.

Gemini is said to favor writers, financiers, Mormons, radio executives, and miscellaneous. Famous Gemini characters include King George V, Queen Mary, Queen Victoria, Jim Tully, Ralph Waldo Emerson, Martha Washington, Gene Tunney, Al Jolson, Pope Pius X, Robert W. Chambers, Jay Gould, Peter the Great, Harriet Beecher Stowe, William Butler Yeats, Walt Whitman, James Montgomery Flagg, Patrick Henry, Ernestine Schumann-Heink, Brigham Young, Saint Boniface, Nero, Gilbert K. Chesterton, and Yvonne, Annette, Cecile, Emilie, and Marie Dionne.

P.S.—Gemini is named after Castor and Pollux, the twin sons of Jupiter and Leda. There never were any such persons, but don't let it worry you.

May 25

"DEAR SIR: I am anxious to obtain a Macgillivray warbler, and what are they, anyhow?

"Outdoors"

Why must you have a Macgillivray warbler, *Outdoors,* when there are dozens and dozens of other kinds of warblers that only an expert can tell apart? There is nothing unusual about the Macgillivray warbler except that it happens to be named after Professor Macgillivray and that it goes *tswee tswee tswee* instead of *peep peep*.

The lutescent warbler, the pileolated, the chestnut-sided, the red-faced, and the knock-kneed warblers—oh, go and get yourself a canary, *Outdoors*. That's what canaries are *for*.

May 26

PROTECTIVE coloration among the animals is another fine subject for vacation study. Take the little yellowish rabbits out where I'm staying. They run like mad when you come anywhere near, then stop dead in their tracks on the glaring white sand beside a clump of green beach grass, apparently in the firm conviction that they are invisible to all and sundry. It works out all right, for their faith in protective coloration is so touching that nobody would dream of disturbing them further.

Maybe my observations aren't quite just to our rabbits, for they were brought from another part of the country where grass may resemble little yellowish rabbits. They don't seem to know they've moved.

May 27

SPEAKING of fish, a few sound facts about the John Dory never hurt anybody. The John Dory is said to have been named after a certain Captain Dory in the French privateer service, who must have been very eccentric, for the fish has a flattish oval body, spiny fins, a huge protruding mouth, and a terrible face, even for a fish. It always looks as though it were perfectly furious at things in general, and very likely that *is* its attitude toward life. As Captain Dory was a rather jolly old pirate, take him by and large, I am inclined to scout the whole story.

The John Dory lives chiefly upon shrimps, herrings, sprats, pilchards, and sand eels. It is olive or brown in color, with yellow bands, and it has a prominent dark spot, ringed with yellow, on each side. Various explanations of these spots have been given, but none of them are much good, and the same things have been said of the haddock. Perhaps we should have concentrated more on the haddock, as it is an American fish in good standing, while the John Dory is found only in the Mediterranean, the Atlantic, around the British Isles, and the Australian seas.

May 28

IS IT my fault if William Pitt the Younger, son of William Pitt the Elder (Lord Chatham), was born at Hayes, near Bromley, Kent, on May 28, 1759? He was a very precocious child. At an age when most English infants would be sticking beans up their nose or asking for a drink of water, he remarked: "I want to speak in the House of Commons, like Papa." And darned if he didn't become Prime Minister when he was only twenty-four. You may have heard his famous saying, as related by an old family retainer: "I think I could eat one of Nicolls's weal pies." What Mr. Pitt actually said, of course, was *veal*, not *weal*.

Mr. Pitt had a passion for office work and never went in for domestic life and that sort of thing. He could have married a young lady with £14,000 a year, but he told her mother: "I am already married to my country." And when another young lady was willing (she was stony broke but beautiful), he said he couldn't afford it, adding: "For my King's and country's sake, I must remain a single man."

Mr. Pitt's niece, Lady Hester Stanhope, always maintained that he would have made an excellent husband because he was so fond of digging in his garden and criticizing ball gowns. Maybe, but he sounds to me like a confirmed old bachelor.

May 29

FOR years I was all wrong about Patrick Henry, who was born at Studley, Hanover County, Virginia, on May 29, 1736, and the person to blame was my Uncle Jasper. You see, Uncle Jasper was quite a card, and one of his favorite stunts was to pull a long face and declaim: "I know not what course others may take; but as for me, give me liberty, or give me death!" This would put everybody in stitches, especially company, and I always laughed a little myself, if he didn't do it too often. He expected it and I took it for granted that it was funny. To this day I don't know why Uncle Jasper had to pick on our great Revolutionary statesman for his jokes—anything for a laugh, I suppose.

Strangely enough, my uncle was just as firm a patriot as Patrick Henry, if not firmer. For instance, Patrick Henry made some cracks about the Constitution that Uncle Jasper would never have dreamed of making, for he wouldn't hear one word said against the Constitution. Patrick Henry didn't even want to adopt the Constitution because he said it would destroy individual liberty and make the President a tyrant—imagine such talk!

I would be the last man on earth to criticize Patrick Henry, but I do think he talked a lot. If this be treason, it's all Uncle Jasper's fault.

THIS is a good day to brush up on Hernando de Soto, the Spanish conquistador. The first time he came to America, De Soto made about $500,000 by helping Pizarro rob Atahualpa, the last of the Incas. Then he went back to Spain and married Isabella de Bobadilla. He could have taken it easy for the rest of his life, but he couldn't let well enough alone. So he came back over here with nine ships, 632 men, 223 horses, and thirteen pigs and landed on the west coast of Florida on May 30, 1539.

De Soto was looking for gold, but all he found was a bag of fresh water pearls which the Indians had spoiled by boring holes in them with red hot needles. He carried these with him for a while and finally lost them in a fire while he was trying to burn up some other Indians. He did, however, discover the Mississippi River, which merely annoyed him because it was

so wide and hard to cross. Finding the Mississippi was something, but even if De Soto had stayed at home, somebody else would have found it sooner or later.

De Soto's reputation has suffered somewhat because he never denied that he was after gold and the more the better. If he had said it was only the sense of achievement that interested him, he might be worth a longer article. As it is, he is only worth a few lines.

May 31

"DEAR SIR: Where is that snippet about crocodiles?
"Louise"

I promised no snippet about crocodiles, *Louise,* and I do hope you are not getting interested in these vicious creatures. Have a tame alligator if you must, but I warn you that crocodiles are something else again. What chance would you stand when Doctor Raymond L. Ditmars himself was almost chased out of a zoo by a captive crocodile? Doctor Ditmars had done practically nothing to it when it gave him a blow with its tail which knocked him down, and then darned if it didn't take after him before he could get up.

Captive alligators will follow their owners around like dogs. But when a crocodile follows you around, it is up to no good.

JUNE

June 1

SINCE this is June 1—all right, then, look it up and see!—birthday honors go to John Masefield, poet laureate of England, who was born on this date in 1878 at Ledbury, Herefordshire. He was appointed laureate in 1930 and a few years later he wrote a very nice ode or something for the jubilee of King George V. John Masefield is pretty well known over here, as he spent some time in our midst, but a few of us might have trouble stating any cogent facts about such former laureates as Nahum Tate, Nicholas Rowe, Laurence Eusden, and H. J. Pye. And that reminds me of Stephen Duck, the favorite poet of Queen Charlotte the Illustrious, wife of King George II.

Queen Charlotte was a patroness of literature. That is, she had a habit of helping the wrong authors to get along, when she wasn't busy trying to pound some sense into George II. So when she heard of Stephen Duck, a self-made rustic bard who had written *The Thresher's Labour* in his spare time, she brought him to town, gave him a pension of thirty pounds a year, and encouraged him to write even worse things. Poor Stephen was made fun of by Swift, Pope, and Gay, who were after pensions themselves.

Among Stephen's surviving verses are some he wrote for the tombstone of Joe Miller, the joke man. They're not so terrible, but they're certainly no good, either—that was his trouble.

June 2

THERE are people who didn't quite catch the name. And who cares? They don't quite catch anything. They never have. Why do they expect it at this late date? Besides, catching a mere name, more or less, isn't likely to help much now. What real good would it do if you told them your name all over again fifteen times and spelled it out for them? It might clear things up for a moment or two, but it won't give them an extra inch above the eyes, will it? So they didn't quite catch the name, eh? Well, the next time they don't quite catch *my* name, I'm going to tell them something that'll hold them for a while—I haven't quite thought it up yet.

June 3

"DEAR SIR: Why do people get married in June, and what is meant by 'creeling the bridegroom'?

"Perplexed"

Oh, sometimes for one reason and sometimes another. There is a pretty general agreement among thinking people that June is a fine month for weddings, and it seems to work out all right. If it didn't, we'd have heard about it by this time. Even the little birds know when it's June, *Perplexed*, and I understand that something of the sort goes on among the sticklebacks, too. In fact, all Nature is more or less in that frame of mind during the month of June, excepting maybe the Trobriand Islanders, who are a law unto themselves.

"Creeling the bridegroom" was once prevalent in the village of Galashiels, Scotland, where every young husband was forced to run around the town with a heavy basket, or creel, of rocks on his back. This went on until about the middle of the nineteenth century, when the inhabitants of Galashiels finally realized that it wasn't especially funny and that it simply made life more difficult for all concerned. So "creeling the bridegroom" stopped, and the wonder is that it ever started. The custom of throwing old shoes after newlyweds is also on the wane. It arose in ancient times, when people had more shoes than they knew what to do with.

June 4

I THINK Mr. G. K. Chesterton was right in wishing that people would stop calling other people morons as much as they do. I'm getting fed up with it myself. Mr. Chesterton said *moron* is the Greek word for fool, which makes it impolite to start with, but there is an even better reason for not using it indiscriminately on anyone. There is the matter of precision. The word *moron* has a definite place in medical circles, meaning a member of the most highly developed group of feebleminded, with a mental age between seven and twelve. Imbeciles are one worse than morons, with a mental age from three to six, and idiots are mentally aged only two years or less.

This being true, as I suppose it is, you can see how easily you might give offense to those you bawl out when you get a little excited. The way I would put it is this: before you go calling your friends this, that, and the other thing, you ought to be sure of your facts. Mr. Chesterton also stated: "It is mainly in America that the fashion has arisen of referring to the average man as a moron."

I don't know about other places, but over here a man has to be dumber than that before he can qualify as a moron. He has to become notorious, if only in his own home, for some signal achievement in dumbness. He has to win his spurs, Mr. Chesterton.

June 5

YOU and I would know very little about political economy if Adam Smith hadn't been born at Kircaldy, Fifeshire, Scotland, on June 5, 1723. His great work is entitled *Inquiry Into the Nature and Causes of the Wealth of Nations,* and at least we know there is such a book. Adam Smith wrote some excellent stuff about rent, wages, profit, capital, labor, and such things. The chief difference between his main doctrine and modern economic thought—well, I mean to say it's a long story and maybe this is not the place to go into it. The fact is that I have not actually read his book word for word, or even skipped through it, much as I may revere it as a classic.

Naturally, we have all read a good many classics, because

we were made to do so at school, but the *Wealth of Nations* is so classic that they don't even *try* to make you read it. And that reminds me that when a friend tremblingly confessed to Charles James Fox that he had never read Adam Smith, the great English statesman replied: "To tell you the truth, nor I either. There is something about all these subjects which passes my comprehension—something so wide that I could never embrace them myself, nor find anyone who did."

Nevertheless, Mr. Fox kept right on telling Parliament how to run the country. He knew that Adam Smith was a great thinker and he just let it go at that.

June 6

"DEAR SIR: Is the cosmos expanding, and what is this Camelopardalis, where Professor Shapley found a new universe?

"Perplexed"

I don't know whether the cosmos is expanding or not—I have all I can do to mind my own business. Camelopardalis is a large but extremely dull constellation between Ursa Major, or the Great Dipper, and Cassiopeia, that zigzag thing that looks like a *W* or an *M*. Camelopardalis is supposed to resemble a Giraffe, or Camelopard, but it really doesn't, unless you happen to be thinking about a Giraffe at the time. For that matter, Ursa Major doesn't look much like a Bear, nor Cassiopeia like a lady named Cassiopeia sitting in a chair.

Perhaps I should add that the Giraffe was once called a Camelopard because it had a head like a Camel and spots like a Pard, although nobody knew exactly what a Pard was, except that it had spots. The truth seems to be that there never was such an animal as the Pard, so it could hardly have had

spots. No, the Pard was *not* the Leopard, for the Leopard was thought to be a cross between Leo the Lion and the Pard.

Some people still insist that the word *Camelopard* is a cross between *Camel* and *Leopard*, which it isn't if you will notice the spelling. They say the Pard and the Leopard were the same thing, but how could that be if the Leopard was a cross between a Lion and a Pard? Who started this, anyway?

June 7

WHEN my friends scold me for never travelling I comfort myself with the thought that Socrates never left Athens. Socrates only smiled when people told him that Athens was all right to visit but they wouldn't live there if you gave them the place. Doctor Samuel Johnson, who also stayed put, except for a few brief trips in his later days, remarked: "When a man is tired of London, he is tired of life; for there is in London all that life can afford."

I don't live in London, but I feel the same way about the place where I do live. Frankly, I wouldn't go across the street to see the Taj Mahal. I haven't decided yet whether this feeling is caused by lack of imagination, pathological fear of losing my suitcase, or just plain dumbness.

June 8

PERSONALLY, I think the clock needs reforming even more than the calendar. I don't seem to have time to do *anything*, let alone read Gibbon's *The Decline and Fall of the Roman Empire* regularly once each year, as some people do—at least they say they do, and I believe that anyone who would say such a thing would be fully capable of doing it. All this spring I've been trying to find time to fix a grapefruit for breakfast, which would be very good for me, but it's simply impossible under present conditions. All I can do is throw it away after a while and get another grapefruit and eventually throw *it* away. What I need is a day and night period of about thirty-six hours.

Of course, there is the matter of daylight and dark to contend with. Science tells us that these are caused by the rotation of the earth on its axis once every twenty-four hours, so any change in that direction is probably out. Well, we could stay up twenty-four hours and sleep twenty-four hours and everything would come out even. That would suit me, but lots of people wouldn't play the game. They'd start getting up at the first crack of dawn and there would go the whole scheme.

Some people have petty minds. They can't take in anything really big.

P.S.—And here's something I want to know. Why is it that every time you look at the clock it's exactly 1:30 a.m.?

June 9

YOU may think authors drink coffee because of the Balzac tradition. I'm not saying that it does any good to drink coffee —still, I wouldn't dream of writing even a casual paragraph for the *Bee Inspector's Journal and Gazette*, to which I sometimes contribute, unless I were full of coffee. Otherwise, I simply wouldn't be at my best.

As for the Balzac tradition, I admit that I often think of Honoré while drinking strong black coffee. But I was drinking coffee like a fiend before I ever heard of Balzac. By the way, I suppose they've exploded the old theory that Balzac died of drinking too much strong black coffee. If not, consider it exploded. Balzac died of overwork. Coffee never killed anybody, but overwork has slain its millions. I think of that, too, while drinking, especially as it takes very little to overwork me.

June 10

MOTHER Nature plays one of her oddest pranks at the expense of the flat fishes.

The very young look just like any other fishes, except that they seem a little flatter than is absolutely necessary. But as the fish grows he swims only on one side, close to the bottom. Why he swims on one side and not on the other is a question that has stumped all our great thinkers. I have a feeling that maybe he could swim on the other side if he tried.

Finally, Mother Nature steps in. The eye on the downward side begins its migration to the top, and eventually both eyes are on top.

In this way, presumably, he can see the bait better, and ends up in the skillet quicker than the more backward fishes. You can't beat old Mother Nature.

June 11

I AM interested, though not very much, in the psychology of those strange people who try to catch the subway when any cat would know that there isn't a chance and would act accordingly. All the facts of life as we know it fairly scream aloud that one cannot catch the subway after the doors have closed for the last time and the train is moving out of the station. One either catches the subway or one doesn't—it's as simple as that, yet they never seem to learn. I wonder what goes on inside these people when it is finally borne in upon them that they are definitely left on the platform again. Do they feel that, anyway, they have tried? Do they keep it up for years, or do they wear themselves out in a hurry? I don't really want to know, but I can't help wondering.

"DEAR SIR: What do you mean alligators are not dangerous? Were you ever chased by one?"

"Outdoors"

No, but perhaps that is because I seldom place myself in a position where I would be likely to be chased by an alligator. Of course, if you stand in front of an alligator when it is going somewhere, you might easily get the impression that it is pursuing you. You may be one of those people who believe that all alligators in the world are lying in wait for them, ready to pounce any instant. The fact is that alligators have their own lives to live. Pull yourself together, *Outdoors*.

I may add that alligators are not always safe when they are cornered or when they are protecting their young. Also, a few alligators are naturally of the vicious type and inclined to re-

sent it when you prod them with a stick. You can find out which ones these are by prodding them. Don't be deceived by the facial expression of alligators. They look as though they were grinning, but they aren't.

In any argument with an alligator it is well to remember that this animal has extremely powerful muscles for closing the jaws—a mechanism which we humans seem to have lost—but it has very weak ones for opening them. The game is to wait until the alligator closes its jaws and then hold them shut with your hands. A still better plan is not to start anything.

June 13

BIRTHDAYS are rather scarce at the moment, unless we drag in Doctor Thomas Arnold, eminent Victorian and headmaster of Rugby School, Warwickshire, England, who was born at West Cowles, Isle of Wight, on June 13, 1795. Doctor Arnold is described in *Tom Brown's Schooldays,* that delightful story by Thomas Hughes, which so few of us have ever read. He has been accused of cruelty because he would flog his pupils whenever they needed it, but that is not all he did by any means. He wrote seventeen volumes of this and that and had ten children, one of whom turned out to be Matthew Arnold, the poet.

Matthew Arnold wrote that lovely thing beginning—oh, you know it as well as I do!

June 14

ON JUNE 14, 1777, our Continental Congress adopted the Stars and Stripes as the Flag of the United States of America. I suppose you know that the first flag of this pattern was made by Mrs. Betsy Ross of Philadelphia, widow of Mr. John Ross —she had been a Miss Griscom before she met John. And I don't want to hear any back-chat to the effect that Betsy Ross and the flag are merely a legend, because I know different.

Personally, I was sent to school as a child and I saw a picture of Betsy actually making the flag. Yes, I know it isn't really a portrait of Mrs. Ross. It's taken from a photograph of a Quaker Lady of Lancaster, but the principle is the same.

June 15

ON JUNE 15, 1752, Benjamin Franklin demonstrated the identity of lightning with electricity by flying a kite during a thunderstorm, and why he wasn't electrocuted at the same time I never *will* understand. The experiment was very picturesque, but if Benjamin Franklin really didn't know that lightning was electricity it does seem as if almost anyone could have told him.

Franklin also invented the lightning rod, the Franklin stove, a smokeless chimney, a bi-focal lens for spectacles, and a chair which became a step-ladder when you turned it over. He was the first to realize that life is often pretty drab for most of us and that if one has a chair that can be made into a step-ladder at a moment's notice—well, it helps.

June 16

MOST authorities insist there is no such thing as an ape language, but Professor Richard L. Garner claimed that monkeys speak "a grammarless system of monosyllables."

In particular, certain chimpanzees of his acquaintance, he said, uttered five distinct sounds, registering the following sentiments: Yes, No, Protest, Satisfaction, and Contempt. To prove his statements, he lived among the animals in a steel cage, accompanied by a recording machine.

He cared more than I do.

June 17

I'VE always been fond of that parlor game where you have to answer a lot of miscellaneous questions on this and that, such as why were the rulers of Babylonia called whatever it was, who was the grandmother of King Whoozes III, and what was the date of something you never heard of before. I'm not perfect at this game, but I was a little shocked at our last session when four out of five players thought the Battle of Bunker Hill was in the Civil War. I didn't say much at the time, but I was fairly sure it was in the *Revolutionary* War, and it turns out I was right.

The Battle of Bunker Hill was fought June 17, 1775. Nobody seems to know just who won, but that will doubtless be cleared up in time. Meanwhile, let's all try to be more definite about things.

June 18

THERE has been a great deal of talk about whether the Duke of Wellington said "Up Guards, and at 'em!" at the Battle of Waterloo, which occurred on June 18, 1815—that much is certain. We all know he denied it shortly after the fight. It seems, however, that nobody would believe him, and finally, in his old age, he admitted it. And nobody knows to this day whether he just did it to save trouble, or whether he got so that he believed it himself, or whether he actually did say it.

Anyway, nobody doubts that Wellington said "Blücher or

night!" at the Battle of Waterloo. I have never envied the Iron Duke for his "Blücher or night!" Personally, I don't think it's very funny.

June 19

I OFTEN wonder about these people who need hardly any sleep. Do they really sleep only six hours each night? And if so, how do they feel the next day? What is their state of mind? Wouldn't they be able to do mental arithmetic a little better if they slept a little longer? Wouldn't they be quicker on the uptake? Or don't they care about that? Some professors once found, by means of experiments lasting six years, that we need eight hours of sleep each night. I have been experimenting longer than that and I find that we need *nine* hours. I would get it, too, if it weren't for seventeen of my neighbors who feel differently about things. Ogden Nash or somebody once spoke of "sleep that knits up the ravell'd sleave of care." There's that, too.

June 20

"DEAR SIR: Please tell me some of Queen Victoria's witty sayings, as I am writing a paper for my club.
"Bookish"

Why don't you try to think up something a little zippier, *Bookish?* The subject you suggest has been regarded as pretty well closed since about 1887, the Diamond Jubilee year. I wouldn't bother to answer you except that today is the anniversary of Queen Victoria's accession to the throne of Great Britain and Ireland—yes, June 20, 1837. Now, let's see! When

she learned of her future greatness, at the age of eleven, she said: "I will be good." That isn't what is technically called wit, but it is a fine saying and will do your club no harm.

I don't know what you'd better do about "We are not amused," for that isn't so awfully witty, either. Queen Victoria first used the expression after she had forced a perspiring young man named Eric to repeat the imitation of herself with which he had been convulsing the court. My own feeling is that her implied criticism of Eric's art was probably just, to put it mildly—and, naturally, Eric was at his worst. Of course, there's also that thing that Mr. Gladstone said, or rather that she said Mr. Gladstone said—or perhaps you could get up a nice paper on current events.

P.S.—Why not leave town?

June 21

NOW that summer is arriving, we shall be seeing a little too much of that tedious and fearfully hackneyed quotation:

> *Sumer is icumen in,*
> *Lhude sing cuccu!*

This bit of quaintness appears to mean that summer has come and the cuckoo is loudly singing and some writer of snippets is hard up for a couple of lines. It is taken from the oldest known English song—and, in my opinion, one of the worst. I have never liked it, but it is probably as good as any other two lines a snippet writer could think up for himself, so why worry?

The cuckoo, somehow, is always breaking into history and folklore as well as literature. Maybe you've heard of the inhabitants of Gotham, Nottinghamshire, who attempted to keep a cuckoo in the village by planting a hedge around the thornbush in which it was singing, so that summer would last forever. Since then the foolishness of Gothamites has been rather taken for granted, perhaps unjustly. Anyway, one of the magistrates of the town declared: "We ween there are more fools pass through Gotham than remain in it."

That's all very well, but the cuckoo got away. And three of the wisest citizens went to sea in a bowl. What about *that?*

June 22

IF YOU believe in astrology, all persons born from June 22 to July 23 are under the Sign of Cancer, the Crab. If you don't, they may strike you as about like the run of other people, allowing for this and that and the way they were brought up. Some of them have highly emotional natures. They are even inclined to jealousy at times, unless they watch themselves. They know that jealousy is absolutely wrong, but they can't seem to help it. Mostly, however, they are fine, upright citizens and very pleasant to meet.

Celebrated persons born under this sign include James McNeill Whistler, David Glasgow Farragut, Walter Hampden, Pearl Buck, Kathleen Norris, Mrs. Pankhurst, Henry Ward Beecher, Otis Skinner, Rexford Guy Tugwell, Giuseppe Garibaldi, William Edgar Borah, Ernest Hemingway, Henry VIII, Isaac Watts, John Quincy Adams, Donald Randall Richberg, Chauncey Olcott, Rembrandt van Ryn, Frank Crowninshield, the Duke of Windsor, Reuben Lucius Goldberg, Irvin Shrewsbury Cobb, Sir William Blackstone, John Paul Jones, and Phineas Taylor Barnum.

Some say these people should marry those born between February 19 and March 21, or between October 24 and November 22. Well, it would all depend, wouldn't it?

June 23

MAYBE I shouldn't bother you with it, but I have long felt that people talk too much, and too loud. I mean practically everybody—people as a species, or whatever you'd call them.

Some of our animal friends are more considerate. A bat's squeak is at the limit of human audibility—some people can never hear it, while a considerable number become deaf to bats as they grow older. That's something to look forward to.

Most armadillos are restricted to a low grunt. Armadillos make affectionate pets, if you need affection that much.

June 24

IT SEEMS there was once a merchant of Venice named Giovanni Caboto, who had three sons named Luigi, Sebastiano, and Santo Caboto. They were all fond of roving about, so they moved to England, where they were known as John and Sebastian Cabot. Then they decided to cross the Atlantic, and they landed on the coast of Newfoundland or Labrador or Cape Breton Island or one of those places on June 24, 1497.

As Christopher Columbus did not reach the mainland of America until eighteen months afterward, the Cabotos were thus the first Europeans to set foot on our continent, unless you count Leif the Lucky, as you certainly should. The English were rather bored with news of America at first, but later they claimed a large share of it on the ground that it had been discovered by two Italians. The Italians and the Norwegians made no such claims. They just came over.

About all the Cabotos got out of their trip was a load of codfish, which they caught off Newfoundland, and £10 presented to them by King Henry VII of England for planting the English flag on American soil at their own expense. Henry VII was very rich and stingy. He saved it all for his son, Henry VIII, who had a marvelous time with it.

June 25

IT SEEMS there were two girls named Lais, and the historians have been mixing them up for centuries. The younger Lais was born in Sicily, the daughter of Timandra, the friend of Alcibiades.

Lais the Elder met Aspasia in Athens, and became a pupil in her salon. Aspasia was about 70 at this point, but she still gave instruction in the arts of elegant conversation and of love. She enjoyed the respect of Socrates, Plato, Antisthenes, and Xenophanes.

Lais graduated with honors in "the art of pleasing" and became one of the greatest of the Greek hetaerae, or companions —a worthy successor to Aspasia herself. After her instructor's death, Lais went to Corinth and gathered about her a number of wealthy young men of "philosophical tendencies." You had to be a rich man to visit Corinth.

Lais soon became the most celebrated of the "erring females." On one occasion, when she found herself in trouble with the authorities, Lais was defended by Diogenes, who won her freedom. She was deeply grateful.

Diogenes's pet doctrine was that "the fewer enjoyments a man had, the happier he was likely to be."

He did approve of a few.

June 26

"DEAR SIR: Who is the leading authority on Atahualpa, the last of the Incas?

"*Constant R.*"

I don't say I'm the *leading* authority, but Atahualpa was the son of Huayna Ccapac, the twelfth Inca of Peru. He usurped the throne, drowning his half-brother, Huascar, the rightful Inca. Then he was imprisoned by Francisco Pizarro, a Spanish conquistador, and bought his freedom by filling a room with gold, and Pizarro murdered him anyway. Afterwards, Pizarro was assassinated by rival Spanish snatchers—as a matter of fact, on June 26, 1541. Pizarro was one of those who have achieved success in later life. He was over sixty when he murdered Atahualpa.

The culture of the Incas has been much admired. They made baskets and pottery and wrote by means of *quipos,* or bundles of knotted cords of various sizes and shapes, if you

would call that culture. We still have an Inca drama written with *quipos*. For all anyone knows, it may be good. Pizarro couldn't read or write, either, so the trouble between him and Atahualpa was something of a toss-up in the matter of culture. By the way, one should study Peru with the aid of a map, as it seems to be on the western side of South America. In my geography I'm pretty sure it was up in the northeast corner. Or was that Bolivia?

June 27

WHEN you go to the beach these days, watch out for Sandpipers. They're up to something. I always supposed Sandpipers were just quaint little birds that ran along the seashore going *peep-peep,* but they'll fly at you sometimes. Maybe the Sandpipers that flew at me were nesting, or maybe they were just feeling rowdy. They didn't scare me for a minute, but I left that part of the beach. Yes, life has its surprises. I never thought I would be chased by a gang of infuriated Sandpipers. I would have bet on it.

June 28

"DEAR SIR: Please devote one of your snippets to Henry VIII, who was born at Greenwich on June 28, 1491. He was not nearly so black as he has been painted, and I think you should bring this out.

"Square Deal"

I know certain historians are trying to prove that Henry VIII was a great statesman and an all-around good fellow, but so far as I am concerned these gentlemen are simply wasting their time. From all I can hear, he was just one more old hypocrite, much overweight, and such he will remain if I have anything to do with it. The whole subject of other people's wives is difficult, but I suppose you will admit that as a husband he left something to be desired.

By the way, I wonder if you know that Henry VIII had a granduncle named Sir Jasper Tudor, who later became Earl of Pembroke and was mixed up in the War of the Roses? He was the son of Owen ap Meredydd, or Owen Tudor, and the widow of Henry V, so he was a half-brother of Henry VI and an uncle of Henry VII. I don't know why, but it has always seemed strange to me, somehow, that Henry VIII should have had a granduncle named Jasper. I'm telling you more to get it off my mind than anything else.

"DEAR SIR: Do you consider the Mona Lisa a portrait of Madonna Lisa del Giocondo, as everybody knows it is, or of Isabella d'Este, as Professor Raymond S. Stites, of Antioch College, said it is?

"Flurried"

I advise you to be careful about these things that everybody knows, *Flurried*. They often prove to be very bad guesses, without a leg to stand on. Nevertheless, I am against Professor Stites's theory, on the ground that Isabella d'Este had a snub nose and the lady portrayed in the Mona Lisa had quite a long nose, if ever I saw a long nose. I don't know how Professor Stites gets around that, but you may be sure he does. Meanwhile, try to get interested in something more important, such as vacation plans.

Isabella d'Este was one of the most charming women of the Italian Renaissance, though not especially noted for her looks. I would say she had a kind face. The real beauty of the Este family was Isabella's sister, Beatrice, who married Lodovico Sforza and became Duchess of Milan, and it just happens that this is her birthday—she was born in Ferrara on June 29, 1475. Alphonse d'Este, the brother of Isabella and Beatrice, was the fourth husband of Lucrezia Borgia, poor fellow.

P.S.—My honest opinion of the Mona Lisa is not for publication. I haven't seen much of it, however. Perhaps it grows on one

June 30

MANY beautiful things have been said about money. One of the best was pulled by a man named L'Estrange, who remarked: "A narrow fortune is a cramp to a great mind." You said something, Mr. L'Estrange!

Mr. J. Brotherton, on the other hand, asserted: "My riches consist not in the extent of my possessions but in the fewness of my wants." It is possible to kid oneself on that subject, and maybe Mr. Brotherton had a touch of that. The Greeks had a proverb: "The wealth of the mind is the only true wealth." The Chinese come right out and admit: "He that is without money might as well be buried in a rice tub with his mouth sewed up."

The Scotch have some ideas, too. "He that winna lout and lift a preen will ne'er be worth a groat" is good conservative doctrine. "A whang off a cut kebbuck's never missed" is still better. If you ask a Scotchman what either of these proverbs means, he'll probably reply: "Mony tynes the half mark whinger." There's no answer to that.

Besides, you wouldn't want to be loved for your money. Or would you?

JULY

July 1

GOTTFRIED WILHELM LEIBNITZ, German philosopher and mathematician, was born at Leipzig on July 1, 1646. It is somewhat difficult to say just what Leibnitz thought about everything, as he didn't write it all down, but he is generally regarded as a great thinker. A great thinker is one who tells us it isn't so. This provides an endless succession of great thinkers, which is very nice for them, but it leaves the rest of us at rather a loose end.

Leibnitz had a lot to do with inventing the differential and the integral calculus, a branch of mathematics the exact nature of which has always eluded me—you have to be that way before you can understand it. He was also fond of talking at some length about what he called *the infinitely little*. One day, after he had tried to explain the infinitely little to Charlotte Sophia, wife of Frederick I of Prussia, she exclaimed to a lady-in-waiting: *"Mon Dieu!* As if I did not know enough of that!"

P.S.—Our philosopher had his practical side, too. He presented Peter the Great with a plan for reorganizing Russia's educational system, a main feature being a salary of 500 rubles per year for himself. He didn't get it.

July 2

ANYWAY, the month of July isn't called *Quintilis* any more, as it was among the old Romans. Seems that in 44 B.C. Mark Antony had the bright idea of changing *Quintilis* to *Julius,* or July, in honor of Julius Caesar, who had done so much for the calendar. Antony chose *Quintilis* because it contained Caesar's birthday and also thirty-one days. The Romans considered odd numbers lucky, so Julius Caesar got a lucky month and two years later he was assassinated. You never can tell how those things will work out.

Not to be outdone, Augustus Caesar, successor to Julius, changed the name of *Sextilis* to August, adding a couple of days so that he would have as many days in his month as Julius had. I forget what happened to Augustus. He probably died in his bed, as he was that sort of person. The Emperor Nero afterwards tried to name the month of April after himself, but nobody paid the slightest attention and April is still April. What we need now is new names for September, October, November, and December.

The Romans had no system of weeks. They named some of their days after festivals, such as *Poplifugia, Furrinalia,* and

Rohigalia, which was named after red dust or mildew, a disease that attacked the grain. They didn't know themselves what *Poplifugia* meant.

July 3

"DEAR SIR: What are you writers doing about a sea-serpent for this summer? Make it a good one while you're at it.
"*Constant R.*"

Sea-serpents are not always invented by writers, as you seem to imagine, *Constant R.* They have also been reported and de-

scribed by persons of the highest respectability, as you would know if you had ever read *Det forste forsog Norges naturlige historie,* or *Natural History of Norway* (Copenhagen, 1752), by Erik Pontoppidan, Bishop of Bergen. Bishop Pontoppidan never actually saw a sea-serpent himself, but he had heard of a great many. His favorite was the Norwegian *Soe Orm,* or sea-snake, which had a head like a horse, with a mane resembling a large mass of floating seaweed—and that is probably what it was.

Bishop Pontoppidan also described the Great Kraken, a species of sea creature beside which the Loch Ness monster was merely a flash in the pan. The Great Kraken was anywhere from a hundred feet to a mile in circumference, according to who saw it. Bishop Pontoppidan regarded it as a myth, but he also thought there might be something in it and he endeavored to extract the nucleus of truth from the story. It is very hard to extract the nucleus of truth from things that just aren't so. Bishop Pontoppidan was constantly running into this problem, but he never gave up.

July 4

LIGHTNING intelligence test: State significance of Fourth of July in fifteen seconds—(a) when, (b) where, (c) what, and (d) why. I thought so. All right then, who invented the cotton gin? Guess the identity of the following persons, all born on the Fourth of July—N-th-niel H--thorne, C-lv-n Cool-dge, Giuseppe G-ribaldi, St-ph-n C-llins F-ster, and George M. Cohan. Well, that's better.

Plenty of other things have happened on the Fourth of July, too. Roger Williams founded Providence at the mouths of the Woonasquatucket and Mooshassuc Rivers on July 4, 1636, after he had been banished from Massachusetts for putting ideas into people's heads. He even said that the soil of North America belonged to the Indians and they ought to be paid for it—imagine! Roger Williams got along splendidly at Providence, except that he missed Boston a little, and he gradually became reconciled to that. He lived to be eighty, a fine old fellow to the last.

Later on, some Quakers, who had also been banished from Massachusetts, went back to Boston and got into trouble. William Robinson and Marmaduke Stevenson were hanged in 1659 for going to Boston twice, and Mrs. Mary Dyer was hanged in 1660 for going three times—she simply couldn't keep away from the place. The hanging of Quakers ceased in 1661, but that didn't help Mrs. Dyer much. As a matter of fact, the Quakers were partly to blame. They would hoot at Governor Endicott as he walked up the street, and Governor Endicott was the type you couldn't hoot at. Moreover, they had been warned time and again, but some people can't take a hint.

July 5

TODAY is known throughout the United States as the day after the Fourth of July. It is also the birthday of Admiral David Glasgow Farragut, as fine an old fellow as ever shouted "Damn the torpedoes! Go ahead!" at the Battle of Mobile Bay, August 5, 1864. Cecil Rhodes was born today, too. He was a very rich man, but I probably couldn't have got a nickel out of him. At least, that's always been my experience with very rich men. Cecil Rhodes did a great deal of good in one way or another. He is also responsible for Rhodes Scholars.

This is also the birthday of Phineas T. Barnum, the circus man, who was born at Bethel, Connecticut, on July 5, 1810. He first became famous by exhibiting Joice Heth, an old colored lady, who said she was a hundred and sixty-one and had been the nurse of George Washington. She told many interesting stories about all she had done for George. "In fact," she said, "I raised him." Well, it turned out that Joice was only seventy and had never met George at all. It was quite a shock to Mr. Barnum.

Mr. Barnum was also a little off on the age of Charles S. Stratton, of Bridgeport, Connecticut, better known as General Tom Thumb. Tom was only five years old when he joined the show, instead of eleven, as advertised. There was nothing phony about Tom's smallness, though. He was only two feet one for a long time and he never grew beyond three feet four. Strangely enough, there was also some doubt as to the height of Jumbo, the celebrated elephant. Jumbo was ten feet nine. Mr. Barnum made it twelve feet six.

Mr. Barnum and Tom Thumb both got into the famous saying lists. You know what Barnum said, but do you know what Tom said to Queen Victoria when she introduced him to the Prince of Wales at Buckingham Palace? He said: "The Prince is taller than I am, but I *feel* as big as anybody." I've heard better, but it struck some people as downright cute.

July 6

THIS is a great day for the Joneses—John Paul Jones was born July 6, 1747. He's the one who said: "I have not begun to fight!" Or maybe he didn't. History consists mostly of things that famous people didn't say. The main thing is to keep these things straight and not get them mixed up with what other famous people didn't say. Review questions: Who never said: "Father, I cannot tell a lie. I did it with my little hatchet"? Just what did John Paul Jones, do, anyway?

And if it hadn't been for Alexander Wilson, ornithologist, who was born at Paisley, Scotland, on July 6, 1766, some of our American birds would have different names, and that would be a great pity. Wilson's Thrush might not sound so poetical if it were called Jones's Thrush—it sounds none too well as it is. As for Wilson's Warbler, it has a hard row to hoe, anyhow, as it is usually mistaken for the Pileolated Warbler or the Golden Pileolated Warbler, which are only subspecies. This must be very discouraging. Wilson's Snipe has similar trouble, most people confusing it with the Long-billed Dowitcher. It is surprising how little some people know about Dowitchers.

Maybe you haven't heard that Mr. Wilson had words with John James Audubon, his rival ornithologist, about a Small-headed Flycatcher. Mr. Audubon said that Mr. Wilson had used his drawing of this bird in a book without acknowledgment. Mr. Wilson replied that he had used his own Small-headed Flycatcher as a model, and a Mr. Ord said he had been present when Mr. Wilson shot it near Philadelphia. It then developed that there probably *is* no such bird as the Small-headed Flycatcher, since nobody has ever seen one from that day on. As sometimes happens, the two scientists seem to have arrived independently at the wrong answer.

July 7

THERE seems to be some confusion as to the exact difference between a summer squash and a vegetable marrow—or maybe I am the only one who can't get it straight. I have looked the subject up many times, and I always finish with the same neat little batch of information: pumpkins, squashes, and vegetable marrows are members of the gourd family (genus *Cucurbita*), the word *squash* comes from the Narragansett Indian word *asquutasquash,* and anybody who doesn't know what a vegetable marrow is will probably go through life in that condition. I am beginning to regard the vegetable marrow as a state of mind.

The English, who know all there is to know about the vegetable marrow, have trouble with the other members of genus *Cucurbita*. One revered authority says the pumpkin is the fruit of a large cucurbitaceous plant, which is true enough, as far as it goes; that in America the name *pumpkin* is applied specifically to particular varieties of *Cucurbita* in distinction from the squash—you'd think it was all our fault, wouldn't you?

July 8

"DEAR SIR: So you think there is no such thing as a sea-serpent, do you? I'll have you know that my grandfather saw several sea-serpents while serving before the mast and was able to describe them in great detail. How do you get around *that*?
"Furious"

I wish I could have known your grandfather, *Furious*. I am sure he was a splendid gentleman and I don't doubt for a moment that his descriptions of sea-serpents grew more and more detailed with each repetition. I like people who have seen sea-serpents much better than the other kind, for they are apt to be jolly companions. Those who have never seen any sea-serpents are often pretty drab, no matter how much they drink. All they can see is the same old things that other people see.

I don't go around telling it, but I once saw a sea-serpent myself while swimming off Jones Beach, Long Island, though it was only a small one—not more than two or three hundred feet long, I should say. Naturally, I swam ashore rather quickly, where I was laughed at by some acquaintances who said they had seen the same thing and that it was merely a school of porpoises. I don't know the first thing about porpoises, but I doubt very much if they look like what I saw. So your grandfather saw *several*, did he?

July 9

ELIAS HOWE, inventor of the sewing machine, was born July 9, 1819, at Spencer, Massachusetts. He received his patent in 1846, after toiling for many years in poverty and distress. And why, my pets, did he keep at it and keep at it until his machine actually sewed? Well, he did it in order to make a whole lot of money—and what's more, he admitted it. Hooray for Elias Howe!

P.S.—He got the money.

July 10

ANY day now is hatching day for Horseshoe Crabs at the beaches—cutest little things you ever saw. In about two weeks they'll have tails and be able to turn upside down. Horseshoe Crabs are not crustaceans. They are marine arachnids and should have become extinct long ago, like the Trilobites and the Sea-Scorpions. Maybe that's why they seem so foolish. Horseshoe Crabs are sometimes made into pipe-racks. You can also make a penwiper out of a stuffed black kitten, but I wish you wouldn't.

July 11

ROBERT BRUCE, king of Scotland, was born July 11, 1274. When he was almost licked by the English and about to give up the struggle, he learned the virtue of perseverance by watching a spider building its web. He then went right out and beat the English and regained his crown.

What happened to the spider is not definitely known, but someone probably stepped on it by mistake. Moral—There's always something.

July 12

"DEAR SIR: The next time Julius Caesar's birthday occurs, please tell me what he actually did about the calendar, instead of just stalling around in your usual way. Give us some definite facts and figures.

"Scholarly"

I have been saving your question until today, as Gaius Julius Caesar was born July 12, 102 B.C. He didn't do as much about the calendar as you might imagine. The real credit should go to Sosigenes of Alexandria, a Greek astronomer and mathematician, who was called in for the brainwork, or what passed for brainwork in those days. Sosigenes had achieved fame by writing a treatise on revolving spheres—without, it must be confessed, knowing a great deal about revolving spheres. Anyway, Caesar grabbed him to ghost his calendar.

Sosigenes was faced by the problem of finding the exact number of days in what is called the tropical year, which is roughly the interval of time between two dates when the sun, in its apparent motion around the ecliptic circle (an imaginary line), attains its greatest angular distance from the celestial equator (another imaginary line)—you asked for it, *Scholarly*. Now this interval contains 365.2422 days, or 365 days, 5 hours, 48 minutes, and 48 seconds. You would hardly expect Sosigenes to figure *that* out, and you would be right. He didn't, and the whole thing had to be done over again.

P.S.—There is still an error of .0003 days per year in our calendar. My advice is to forget it.

July 13

IT'S AMAZING how many superstitions one encounters among otherwise intelligent people. I know a lady who practically has a fit if a black cat crosses her path. Yet nothing very terrible ever happened to me after a black cat crossed my path. I wish I could say the same for tortoise-shell cats.

Superstition is plain, downright ignorance. Such beliefs merely shackle the mind and hold you back. Of course, if you break a leg on account of a tortoise-shell cat, that would shackle you even worse, so I keep my eye on them just in case.

One of my friends carries a rabbit's left hind foot in his pocket the year round. He gets along very well and he lays it all to this charm. He doesn't seem to know that in order to be any good the rabbit must be killed in a churchyard at midnight in the dark of the moon. He's simply a victim of ignorance.

Any child should know that breaking a mirror couldn't possibly cause seven years of bad luck, though I'd as soon not break one myself. I went into that scientifically once by breaking a mirror and keeping track of my luck for the next seven years. The experiment didn't prove much, really. I hadn't been so awfully lucky before that, either.

July 14

THIS is the birthday of the typewriter. The first efficient model was patented July 14, 1868, by Christopher Latham Sholes, Carlos Glidden, and Samuel Soule, of Milwaukee. The typewriter is a boon to authors, as it enables them to say more and mean less than any other invention. Before 1868 authorship involved a great deal of hard work and a lot of time. Today this sort of thing can be turned out in practically nothing flat. That makes it nice for authors.

July 15

PERSONALLY, I'm going to celebrate the birthday of Inigo Jones, who arrived on July 15, 1573, in London. Inigo came of poorish parents and when a lad was apprenticed to a joiner, or maker of furniture, which he didn't like a bit. So he went to Italy and studied art and became the greatest architect in England—Sir Christopher Wren wasn't born yet.

He has been kidded a little for examining into the origin of Stonehenge and deciding that it might have been made by the Druids and then again it might be the work of the Romans. As that was about what everybody else thought at the time, the investigation didn't amount to much, it is true. But we *still* don't know who built Stonehenge, or what it was for, so why pick on Inigo?

July 16

SIR Joshua Reynolds, great English painter, was born at Plympton Earl, Devonshire, on guess what date in 1723— yes, July 16! One of his pictures, you know, is *The Age of Innocence*, that little girl with a blue sash and bare toes. Another—well, I'm afraid I was going to mention the *Blue Boy,* but that seems to have been painted by Gainsborough.

Sir Joshua also founded a literary club with Doctor Samuel Johnson, Edmund Burke, and some others such as Sir John Hawkins, who proved to be a mistake and had to be frozen out. Sir John once refused pointblank to pay his share of the supper bill, whereupon Doctor Johnson observed: "Sir John, Sir, is a very *unclubable* man." The strange thing was that Sir John had all kinds of money—at least, his wife had.

July 17

I HAVE never quite approved of Charlotte Corday, who murdered Jean Paul Marat in his bath during the French Revolution. Not that I ever liked Marat, who was pretty vicious himself. I can see Charlotte's side of it, too; she thought she was doing good, and she didn't mind attracting a little attention at the same time. But I simply can't stand ladies who go barging into other people's bathrooms with kitchen knives—they ought to draw a line somewhere. I'd forgotten the worst angle of the crime until I saw it in the waxworks at Coney Island. Marat was wedged into a trick bathtub shaped

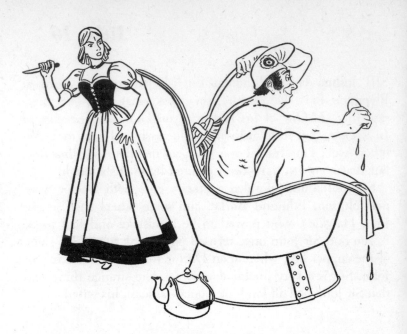

like a big shoe and he couldn't possibly have put up a fight. He hadn't a chance. By the way, Charlotte was guillotined on July 17, 1793.

July 18

THESE are the days to watch your young cabbage. Once arrived at maturity, cabbage is as sturdy a vegetable as the next, but a lot of it never grows up. All the cabbage I ever had anything to do with began looking perfectly terrible about July 18. It was just a bunch of loose leaves with no head to speak of, and the leaves were full of holes. It does seem as though one should be able to grow cabbage like other people's. I don't know what you ought to do about it—but do *something*.

July 19

ON THIS date in 1929 the Russians were threatening the Chinese, the weevils were menacing the Mississippi Valley, *Pro Bono Publico* was writing to the papers about the Eighteenth Amendment, and the radio programs were awful. President Hoover was fishing in the Blue Ridge Mountains, Governor Franklin D. Roosevelt of New York was on the job, and the leading American bird was the Bald Eagle. People with money had a great deal of it, and the rest of us were about as usual. Who says there's no progress?

July 20

FRANCESCO DI PETRACCO, afterwards known as Francesco Petrarca, or Petrarch, great Italian poet, was born at Arezzo on July 20, 1304. He might have been born in Florence, but his father and mother were Ghibellines and had been driven away from there by the Guelphs. The Guelphs and the Ghibellines were political parties and were very important in history. In those days it was possible to tell them apart, but this cannot be done any more—it is one of the lost arts. Petrarch wrote some wonderful poems about a lady named Laura, who inspired him artistically during the greater part of his career. Some people say that Petrarch was not really in love with Laura, as he hardly knew her by sight. But if he *thought* he was, doesn't it come to about the same thing?

"DEAR SIR: I need some information on moths, but I suppose you know nothing about them.

"June Bride"

That's where you're wrong, *June Bride*, for I've just been brushing up on moths. Three kinds that should interest you are the Case-making Clothes Moth (*Tinea pellionella*), the Webbing Clothes Moth (*Tineola biselliella*), and the Tapestry Moth (*Trichophaga tapetzella*). The proper procedure with all three is about the same. You snatch at them with your fist as they flutter around the room, since they seldom alight and are therefore difficult to swat. You practically never catch them, but you give them pause. It makes them think. Moth-snatching makes a lively game for these summer evenings.

The actual moths you snatch at, of course, do not eat your winter things, but they are all getting ready to have children, or larvae, which feed upon woolens, carpets, feathers, furs, upholstery, college pennants, and miscellaneous. These larvae will eat almost anything except ancient Tuxedos that really ought to be eaten. A friend of mine, however, succeeded in losing his old Tuxedo by packing it in a moth-proof box. The box proved 100 per cent effective. Not a moth escaped. They stayed right there in the Tuxedo and had a wonderful time.

July 22

SATURN and its rings are all right, but give me Jupiter and its moons for real downright enjoyment. Jupiter, you know, is the largest planet in our solar system, larger than all the others combined. It's 87,225 miles in diameter and 1,312 times the bulk of the earth, though much less dense. Doctor Henry Norris Russell of Princeton said that planets much larger than Jupiter are impossible because of something I didn't quite catch, so when you look at it through one of those street telescopes you can be sure you're getting your money's worth. Jupiter has nine moons, but the only ones you can see in an ordinary telescope are Io, Europa, Ganymede, and Callisto. The others are much smaller and you can't see them for a nickel—what did you expect?

July 23

"DEAR SIR: In your recent snippet on household moths you utterly neglected to mention the Buffalo Moth. How could you?

"Admirer"

Because the Buffalo Moth (*Anthrenus scrophulariae*) is not a moth, but a beetle, in spite of its name. The young, or larvae, of these insects used to infest the great herds of Buffalo in the Old West until the Buffalo became practically extinct, when they switched to carpet for one reason or another. Now that carpet is also becoming extinct I don't know what their plans are, but I have a feeling they'll get along somehow.

Nor do I know why the Buffalo Moth has chosen to identify itself so oddly with lost causes and vain ideals. Just its way, I suppose.

ARE you Bolivar-conscious? Well, this is the birthday of Simon Bolivar, who invented South American revolutions. Bolivar freed Venezuela, Colombia, Ecuador, Panama, Peru, and Bolivia from Spain. He devoted his life to this task and died in 1830, and there are statues of him in Caracas, Bogota, and Lima. The Bolivians use bolivianos for money. The Venezuelans use bolivars. *Now* are you Bolivar-conscious?

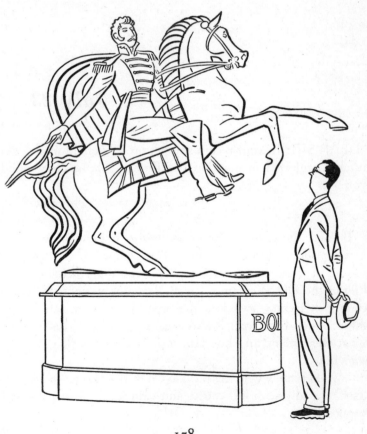

July 25

"DEAR SIR: Kindly write something about the *cedilla,* the little mark that is sometimes placed under the letter *c* to show that it is to be pronounced like the letter *s,* as in façade.

"Worried"

You seem to know more about it than I do, so why worry? Millions of people have lived happy and useful lives without ever hearing of the *cedilla,* let alone mastering it in all its detail. In times like these you should be able to get along very well without *cedillas,* and that goes for façades, too. If the *cedilla* is all you have to worry about, you're lucky. You might take a day off, however, and worry about the following: Who was the Man in the Iron Mask? Where is the Lost Dauphin? What becomes of all the pins? Where are the snows of yesteryear? Let me know how you get along.

July 26

I DON'T like to complain, but the partial eclipse of the moon on July 26, 1934, was about the last straw. It was totally invisible in the Eastern states, where most of the eclipse fans live. When it began, at 4:50 A.M., Eastern Standard Time, it was visible in some of the Western states and at certain strategic points in the Antarctic Ocean, where few people care for eclipses. It finished somewhere in Central Asia, where *nobody* cares. What kind of an eclipse is that, anyway?

July 27

ON JULY 27, 1844, John Dalton, founder of the Atomic Theory, passed away in Manchester, England, but his work goes marching on. He thought the atom was the smallest imaginable particle of matter, which it isn't. We now imagine a nucleus and some electrons inside the atom, and some people can even imagine neutrons and protons.

Doctor Dalton went to church twice each Sunday, and he said he liked to take his Saturday in the middle of the week. He was also afflicted with color-blindness, or Daltonism, as it was called after he wrote it up. He read few books and talked hardly at all. When he said anything, he said a mouthful.

July 28

ON THIS date in 1929 it was Sunday and the maximum temperature in New York City was 92 degrees. Two hundred children got lost at Coney Island and were returned to their parents a few minutes later. The Yankees beat the St. Louis Browns, 7 to 6, and guess who won the game with a homer in the twelfth? Yep—Babe Ruth. Crops were suffering from a long dry spell, and the next day it rained. A book called *The Art of Thinking* was a national best seller. So *that* problem was solved.

July 29

"DEAR SIR: Why don't you mention the planet Venus once in a while instead of raving about Mars and Pluto and such small fry?

"Justice"

There is something in what you say, *Justice*. Venus is one of our most deserving planets and I am delighted to give her a testimonial. If I have not done so before, it is because I have always felt that she could take care of herself. Since Venus is the brightest object in the sky, excepting maybe the moon, there is very little chance that she will be overlooked. Venus was known to the ancients and she still attracts a lot of attention, especially when she is evening star. Hardly an evening passes that somebody doesn't point up at her and exclaim: "What is *that*?"

July 30

ON THIS date in 1930 the Prince of Wales flew to Belgium, President Hoover went to a baseball game, and Doctor Davidson Black announced the discovery of the second Peking Man skull, one of the oldest fossils ever—the first Peking Man skull was that of a woman and was the thicker of the two. A great many people fell asleep while taking sun-baths, got badly burned, and swore they would never do *that* again. Henry Ford, just sixty-seven years old, told reporters that his favorite poem was *Maud Muller,* and Edward "Red" Githens, of Camden, New Jersey, was still aloft after shattering all tree-sitting records with a mark of 336 hours. And some of us had a lot to learn.

THIS is the birthday of John Ericsson, the Swedish inventor who designed the famous Civil War ship, the *Monitor*. Of course you know all about the battle of the *Monitor* and the *Merrimac*, the first conflict between ironclad vessels. That is, you know all about it except which was which, and what happened, and why. Well, the *Monitor*, on the Union side, was the one that the Confederates called a cheesebox on a raft because it had a revolving turret, and the fight was a draw. Doesn't that bring it all back?

AUGUST

August 1

JEAN Baptiste Pierre Antoine de Monet, Chevalier de Lamarck, distinguished French scientist, was born at Bazantin, Picardy, on August 1, 1744. He was the first person to point out that animals without backbones should be classed as invertebrates. It does seem as though the other scientists should have known that, but they didn't—for instance, they classed lizards as insects. Lamarck is better known for his belief in the inheritance of acquired characters. He thought the children of a skillful pianist would inherit some of the skill, but the fact is they often hate the piano and even refuse to practice. Lamarck wrote some important books, cleared up a great many things, and is still a great name in science. He lived to be eighty-five and was buried in the Potter's Field.

August 2

SPEAKING of heat, John Tyndall, British scientist, was born in County Carlow, Ireland, on August 2, 1820. He wrote a book which explained the mechanical theory of heat and did a great deal for the subject. They've got heat down to a fine point now, the gist of it being that heat and molecular motion are one and the same thing. This is rather hard to grasp if you have always thought of heat as just something hot, but a little fundamental brainwork will straighten it out. For instance, when you heat a molecule—no, that isn't quite the idea. In fact, the whole problem of thermodynamics would make a fine little essay for winter reading.

August 3

IN SOME parts of the world crickets are kept in wire cages, much as we keep canaries. It would be fine to have both. Then the crickets could start screeching as soon as the canaries stopped.

Cricket experts divide crickets into many species of the genus *Gryllus*. They measure great numbers of crickets at various strategic points and classify them accordingly. They then have several species and a vast amount of data left over that nobody seems to want.

Professor Lockhead, some years ago, was unable to see any difference between *Gryllus abbreviatus* and *Gryllus pennsylvanicus*. I can't see any difference between any of them, only some are meaner and louder. A really mean cricket is mean clear through.

August 4

ON THIS date in 1929 electrical workers at Guayaquil, Ecuador, were threatening to strike because they couldn't cash their pay checks because the bank employees were striking. Yee Sun, a Hip Sing Tong member, was shot in Chicago; King George V was feeling better after his operation; and the Graf Zeppelin arrived at Lakehurst, New Jersey, from Europe with nineteen passengers, a stowaway named Albert Buchsow, a gorilla named Susi, a chimpanzee named Louis, and 593 canaries, probably named Dick. Doesn't it beat all?

August 5

WELL, the Dog-Days are almost over now, if that's any comfort—they're supposed to last from about July 3 to about August 11. The Dog-Days were named by the ancients on the theory that midsummer heat is partly caused by Sirius, the Greater Dog-Star, or maybe by Procyon, the Lesser Dog-Star, which rise practically with the sun around this time of year and thus add to its general warmth.

There's nothing in it. Sirius is 8.8 light years away from us and Procyon is still farther, and neither one raises the temperature so you could notice it. The ancients got a great many things all balled up. They did know, however, when they were hot.

"DEAR SIR: What do you think of celebrities who hide from photographers and run away from us autograph fans?

"Disgusted"

I suppose that's another crack at Alfred, Lord Tennyson, who had to build a high fence around his house at Farringford, on the Isle of Wight, to keep out the tourists who hounded him day and night with cameras and autograph albums. I'm on his side. I don't believe it helped much to have a lot of strangers climbing the fence, peering through cracks, snapping pictures, and yelling: "That's him!" while he was trying to get his mind on the *Idylls of the King*. And now that the subject has come up, Tennyson was born at Somersby, Lincolnshire, on August 6, 1809.

August 7

ON AUGUST 7, 480 B.C., what Greek hero attempted to hold the Pass of Thermopylae against the whole Persian army with three hundred Spartans and a few Thebans and Thespians? Yes, it was Leonidas, King of Sparta—that's an easy one. And now if you're trying to think who it was that ran twenty-two miles to Athens with news of the battle, that had nothing to do with Thermopylae. That was after the Battle of Marathon, and the fellow's name was Pheidippides. Some writers say his right name was Philippides and that it is vulgar to call him Pheidippides. You'll have to use your own judgment about that—it's all Greek to me.

August 8

MOTHER Nature is having the time of her life these days. Elderberries are ripe, if you like them, and the young black-snakes are emerging from their eggs, so that we'll all be tripping over them soon. Poison ivy flourishes everywhere—it looks like a bumper crop again. The ragweed is doing nicely, too. Most of the birds have quieted down, but the nights are filled with the songs of billions of insects, some of which bite. Any minute now the crickets will move into the house and stay there until frost. Oh, well!

August 9

IZAAK Walton, author of *The Compleat Angler*, was born in Stafford, England, on August 9, 1593. He knew a great deal about fish, although he was mistaken in thinking that infant pike are bred from pickerel weed by spontaneous combustion—it isn't as simple as all that. He has been accused of cruelty to bait, because he advises us to put a frog on the hook "as though you loved him; that is, harm him as little as you may possibly, that he may live the longer." Why isn't that kindness to frogs?

Besides, most of the minnows Walton used for bait were salted. He also used an artificial minnow. Almost everybody loved Izaak Walton, but Lord Byron called him "a quaint old cruel coxcomb." That's nothing to what Lord Byron has been called.

August 10

ON THIS date in 1929 a porcupine saved the situation for a lady and seven children who had been lost in the woods while picking berries near North Bay, Ontario. The porcupine wounded the lady's dog in the nose, the dog started for home, and the berry pickers followed. A festival in honor of watermelon began in Rome, and at West Branch, Iowa, a granite boulder was dedicated on the spot where President Herbert Hoover was born. Otherwise, it was kind of an off day.

August 11

YOU might think a plant named *Ambrosia artemisiaefolia* would be quite a plant, but it's only the common ragweed, otherwise called wild tansy, hogweed, bitterweed, hayweed, and stammerwort. Nobody loves the common ragweed because it is responsible for many cases of hay fever, and hay fever is not much fun. In the effort to do a little good by way of helping hay-fever victims, I have been destroying a great deal of ragweed around my summer shack. Or rather, the man who told me it was ragweed had evidently never seen any ragweed. Now I may never know what it was I destroyed, and I suppose it's too late to worry. Well, I was only trying to do good! And it *might* have been ragweed, mightn't it?

August 12

ACCORDING to astrology, persons born between July 24 and August 23 are under the the sign of Leo the Lion. Leo persons are very nice as a rule, but when they are bad they are horrid. They're inclined to worry when they're broke and to feel better at other times.

Leo children often refuse to eat their spinach. Celebrated Leo persons include George Bernard Shaw, Henry Ford, Benito Mussolini, Herbert Hoover, and Ethel Barrymore. Well, it takes all kinds!

August 13

IT SEEMS the planet Mercury is in perihelion today. That is, it's as near the sun as it ever gets, or about 28,550,000 miles, instead of 43,350,000 miles, as it is in aphelion. Mercury's mean distance from *us* is 93,000,000 miles and its diameter is 3,100 miles. Isn't it strange that the farther away a thing is, the more we know about it?

If you have never seen the planet Mercury, don't let it get you down. Copernicus never did, either, and he lived to a ripe old age.

August 14

IF WE *must* have anecdotes, I always say it might as well be the one about Queen Elizabeth and Sir Mary Cholmondeley.

It seems there was a certain Lady Mary Cholmondeley, the wife of Sir Hugh Cholmondeley, and she was known as "the bold lady of Cheshire" because she was always speaking her mind. So when the Spanish Armada started for England, she said such brave things about how it would surely be licked to a frazzle that Queen Elizabeth up and knighted her on the spot, and Sir Mary she remained to the end of her days. Well, England defeated the Armada, with the aid of a gale of wind, and just a week later Drake, Hawkins, and Howard went back to London and broke training, and *that* was in mid-August, 1588.

August 15

THIS is the birthday of Napoleon Bonaparte, Sir Walter Scott, Thomas de Quincey, and Walter Hines Page. Little boys born today are likely to become soldiers, novelists, essayists, ambassadors, spring poets, tea tasters, bee inspectors, or street car conductors.

Most of the little girls will be very pretty, but sixty-seven per cent of them will say "*those* sort of things," and nothing will stop them. At least, nothing has so far.

August 16

AS YOU all used to know when you were in school, Colonel John Stark was the hero of the Battle of Bennington, which took place on August 16, 1777, near Bennington, Vermont —though some say it was really over the border in Hoosic, New York. I was brought up to believe that just before the fight with the Hessians, Colonel Stark addressed to his militiamen the following words: "Tonight the American flag floats from yonder hill or Molly Stark sleeps a widow." Which is exactly the way a famous saying ought to sound. But now the historians have tamed it down to the following comparatively dumb remark: "You must beat them or Molly Stark is a widow tonight."

I do wish they could leave a swell quotation alone. Anyway, it was a great day for the Starks.

August 17

HOORAY for Davy Crockett, Indian fighter, bear hunter, Congressman, and all-around good fellow, who was born August 17, 1786, on the banks of the Nolichucky River in Tennessee, near what is now Rogersville, Hawkins County. He attended school for only six months and never quite got the hang of it. He said that spelling was contrary to nature, which strikes me as truer and truer the more I think it over —and I would put long division in the same class, especially where there are decimals. He also swore by the motto: Be sure you're right, then go ahead. That is not as wise as it sounds, because most people are sure they're right and you know the answer.

August 18

AT THIS time in 1929 the thermometer registered 100 degrees in Oklahoma City and Abiline, 96 degrees in San Antonio and Phoenix, and 84 degrees in Los Angeles. In Little America, Antarctica, Commander Byrd and his men were caught in a blizzard at 7 degrees below zero. Some people have all the luck. Officials of the New York State Insurance Fund announced that a gardener had poisoned his wounded ankle by rubbing it against a daffodil. That's what started all this daffodil poisoning.

August 19

THERE are people who stick so many pins into new shirts that by the time you've got them out the shirts aren't new any more. There are people who wrap up this summer's straw hats and save them for next summer, and it's really none of my business. There are people who think hay fever is all in your head. There are people who say: "Well, Bill, you've certainly put on quite a bit of weight these last few years—you certainly have!"

There are people who tell you to look on the bright side. It might be worth trying, at that.

August 20

THAT bird you keep hearing is probably a Song Sparrow, one of the few birds still singing at this time of year. There are twenty-some species of Song Sparrows distributed throughout the United States and Canada, so nobody need be without one. There are dozens of other kinds of sparrows. They sing, too.

Song Sparrows love to hang around houses and sing at all hours of the day and sometimes at night. They keep this up until November 1. You could move to Alaska, but there are Song Sparrows there, too.

"DEAR SIR: How can I get my husband to stop reading the paper at breakfast? I simply hate it.

"Housewife"

. As your husband doubtless reads the paper at breakfast in order to find out what is going on in the world and thus fit himself for his daily grind at the office, you might ask him to give up his business or profession. Tell him you married him for himself alone and that you don't care a bit whether he makes any money or not. If you feel strongly enough on the subject, you might let him know in a tactful way that you will go out and earn the living if he will only give up this annoying habit. Maybe you can work it so there won't *be* any breakfast. That might solve your problem.

August 22

MAYBE we'd all feel better if we indulged in a few kindly thoughts about goldenrod, one of the loveliest flowers we have, though some people call it a weed. Goldenrod is often unjustly blamed for cases of hay fever that are actually caused by ragweed, timothy, cat fur, and what not. Indeed, some doctors say that goldenrod is practically innocent, since it is pollinated by bees and doesn't spread its pollen in the air at all. I shouldn't like to decide this question, as lots of people start sneezing at the mere sight of goldenrod. Perhaps it doesn't give them hay fever, but it gives them something else that produces the same results. Personally, I love the gorgeous goldenrod, but there is a certain species of timothy I'd like to get even with.

August 23

COMMODORE Oliver Hazard Perry was born August 23, 1785, although he was not a commodore at the time. He defeated the British at the Battle of Lake Erie in 1813, and immediately wrote the following note to General William Henry Harrison on the back of an old envelope: "We have met the enemy and they are ours!"

After that, hundreds of babies were named Oliver Hazard Perry Something-or-other. There were dozens of O. H. P. Joneses alone. You don't see that so much any more.

August 24

"DEAR SIR: What can I do about crickets in the home?
"Sleepless"

Life has taught me that the less one does about crickets in the home the better for all concerned. I hold no brief for helping animals of any kind, but one simply can't spend every night hunting a cricket with a flashlight and an old shoe. Statistics prove that the average cricket is faster than the human eye, even if you know where it is, so all you get is a sense of defeat, not to mention the wear and tear. Besides, some say it's unlucky to kill a cricket. The proper procedure is to carry it some distance from the house, hurry back to bed, and try to get some sleep before it returns. Anyway, sleep isn't everything.

August 25

THE time will come when the human race has evolved so that dessert will always be strawberry shortcake. What else? And it can't come soon enough. Of course, if you wanted to make a pig of yourself, you could always top it off with a pint of vanilla ice cream, though certain people may feel that a quart is more suitable.

I hate to mention it, but let's not rule out animal crackers, one of my favorite foods. After all, it isn't every day you can bite off the head of a lion.

August 26

"DEAR SIR: You won't remember the summer of 1920, but I am the girl who used to read your collection of books on psychoanalysis at High Hill Beach. What fun we had, talking of nothing but the libido and paranoia and all those exciting things. Why is it that mystery writers have taken up psychology only these last few years? Hadn't they heard of it before?

"Gwenn"

Of course I remember 1920. Weren't the green flies awful that summer? I have just read your questions over the phone to Miss X, author of several psychological mysteries, and she tells me the public was not ready for psychology until a few years back, when she wrote her first one. She was ready but nobody else was, get it?

I have reason to suspect that she first heard of psychology in 1945, when she attended a movie in which it was featured. A lot of mystery authors saw that picture.

August 27

IN Upper Bavaria these days you may still find carp spawning this late in the season. Most carp spawn in May, June, or July. In Sicily and Algeria they often get in the mood and spawn as early as April. There's no holding some carp.

In the Orient, the carp has been domesticated and is held in high esteem. Elsewhere, there are people who wouldn't mind at all if the carp became extinct. That's hardly likely, though—in one pond four males and three females produced 110,000 young in one year. And they were just ordinary carp. That will give you an idea.

August 28

A FORMER acquaintance of mine once launched into a defense of fried bananas, just before she became a former acquaintance. At least, she said, you can put lemon juice on them. So you can. I hadn't realized that!

You can also put creosote on them. Or formaldehyde. Or chloride of lime.

A nation that fries bananas cannot long endure.

August 29

"DEAR SIR: What ancient poet was so thin that he had to wear lead in his shoes to keep from blowing away? Does the gemsbok ever drink water, and what are the Eugubine Tables?

"Ambitious"

Take it easy, *Ambitious.* Rome wasn't built in a day. I have not heard of the poet you mention, so you can be pretty sure there *was* no such person. If there was, he probably had some friends who started the story as a joke, and feeble enough it is. Besides, a poet as thin as that would not be able to carry the lead around.

Some scientists say that the gemsbok, a large South African antelope, never drinks water. This simply means that these scientists have never happened to see a gemsbok drinking water. I always use my own judgment in problems pertaining to the gemsbok.

As for the Eugubine Tables, they are certain tables of Eugubine origin; or, rather, one might say, there is a considerable difference of opinion about their true nature and significance. Really, *Ambitious*, I don't believe it would do you a bit of good to learn about the Eugubine Tables, and if you think I don't know what they are myself, go on and think it. Where did year hear about them, anyway?

Later—The poet with the lead in his shoes seems to have been Philetas of Cos. I still can't see that it matters.

August 30

I DON'T know whether you realized it or not but there are still some sea elephants around. Some people know them as elephant seals. The males have long pendulous noses and

sometimes achieve a girth of 15 or 16 feet. They are the largest of all seals, but the ordinary seal is twenty times as smart.

Sea elephants are inclined to be good-natured. Their main interest seems to be food, but the males become interested in the females from time to time, and vice versa. It's surprising how long some of the old fellows retain their *joie de vivre*.

All sea elephants want out of life is plenty of fish and a chance to doze in the sun. I'd settle for that myself.

"DEAR SIR: How can I clean an alabaster bust that has been lying around in the attic for years?

"Daisy"

I must say your question catches me a trifle unprepared on a subject to which I am not, after all, an utter stranger. I had occasion to observe a great many alabaster busts in the town where I grew up. My Aunt Elizabeth had a lovely one. So had several young ladies on my regular calling list, and I assure you they were all in splendid condition, always. I really never inquired how they kept them that way, or I might be of more help to you in your little difficulty.

Personally, I am a great believer in soap and water, but I seem to remember having read somewhere that soap has a tendency to discolor alabaster ornaments, or was it marble? I suggest that you try it, anyway, first in small areas where any damage might not be too noticeable, employing for the purpose a very mild, lukewarm suds and a soft cloth. Rinse thoroughly and dry with a clean towel, if you have one in the house.

I may add, in case you have forgotten how it used to look, that you needn't worry if a yellowish tint results from your efforts. Some alabaster busts are naturally yellowish, especially the older ones, and here we seem to be dealing with a real antique. On the other hand, if it turns bright green or something equally unpresentable, like red and blue polka dots, you can always take it back to the attic.

SEPTEMBER

September 1

ASTROLOGERS tell us that persons born between August 24 and September 23 are under the Sign of Virgo. Such persons often possess cold natures until they get really interested —then there's no stopping them. They are sometimes behind in their rent but they always pay up in the long run. They need a good deal of sympathy and plenty of orange juice. Famous Virgo persons include General Pershing, Saint Augustine, Robert Benchley, Theodore Dreiser, Savonarola, C. K. G. Billings, Queen Elizabeth, H. L. Mencken, Rex Beach, and Queen Wilhelmina. Nice weather we're having.

September 2

"DEAR SIR: What is the lowdown on that mousetrap quotation, anyway?

"Vox Pop"

I suppose you're thinking of Ralph Waldo Emerson's assertion that if a man can make a better mousetrap than any other man, the world will beat a path to his door. There are several versions of this crack, the best being by an uncle of mine, who said that if a man can make a better mousetrap than any other man, the world will beat a path to the ten-cent store. This was rather a sore point with him, as he had spent many years making a perpetual-motion machine which he afterward tried to market as a mousetrap, and nothing came of it. Naturally, he was a little embittered.

September 3

DON'T let it get you down, but September 3 is a tricky date —you can't always count on it. For instance, there simply wasn't any September 3 in 1752, at least in England, for that was the time they changed the calendar from Old Style to New Style by ruling that the day after September 2 should be September 14. That is, they adopted the Gregorian calendar to replace the Julian calendar, because they had been eleven days behind everybody else for about a hundred and seventy years. They're doing a little better now.

Some people got the impression that their lives had been shortened eleven days by Act of Parliament, and some held that all persons whose birthdays fell between September 2 and September 14 were legally dead. They would run after

186

Henry Pelham, the Prime Minister, and shout: "Who stole the eleven days?"

This gave poor Mr. Pelham a bad case of nerves, for if there was any one thing he didn't like to have shouted at him it was any form of the verb "to steal." There had been a good deal of talk.

The fact is that Lord Chesterfield was largely responsible for the change. The letters he received from the Marquise de Monconseil, one of his French cronies, were naturally dated according to the Gregorian calendar, or eleven days ahead of the Julian calendar used by the English. Lord Chesterfield always felt as though he had received them the day before they were written.

So he went into the matter, introduced a bill in Parliament, and put it over—all on account of the lady. Anyway, that's what he told the Marquise de Monconseil, who dearly loved a compliment now and then, as who doesn't. The real reason was that Lord Chesterfield couldn't bear to be eleven days behind the times.

I believe we're having September 3 today, but you never can tell.

September 4

IT WON'T be long before the bumblebees wind up their affairs for the season, and I'll be just as well pleased. Any time now you may expect the nuptial flight of the young queens and the males. Then the males will perish and the young queens will go to sleep for the winter. The queens will wake up in the spring and start it all over again, but meanwhile we'll have things our own way.

Some people will tell you that bumblebees ask only to be let alone and that they will not sting you unless you poke them with a stick, take after them with a fly-swatter, or attempt to put them into bottles.

The main weakness of this theory is that I know different. I once stepped on a bumblebee nest. Perhaps the bumblebees were just trying to be sociable, because they belong to the Social Hymenoptera. I suppose that wasn't letting them alone, in the strict meaning of the words.

Some very startling things have been discovered by bumblebee scholars. Sir John Lubbock once found that a bee visited his room for honey fifty-nine times between 6:55 A.M. and 7:15 P.M., but I think that was a honey bee. I forget now what it proved, except that the bee finally decided to call it a day. Bees are indeed wonderful, but they're not my favorite creatures. Say what you will, they're insects.

September 5

IT MAY or may not thrill you to learn that the planet Saturn is now practically in our midst. That is, it never gets nearer than 745,000,000 miles, but it's appearing in the southeastern sky at a reasonable hour these evenings—say, around nine or ten o'clock.

You'll find Saturn in the constellation of Aquarius, the Water-Bearer, which is one of the meanest of all constellations to identify, unless you've made a life work of it. Aquarius is sort of south and west of the great square of Pegasus, the Flying Horse. If you draw an imaginary line through the two large upper stars of Pegasus and prolong it downward the same distance, you'll wind up a bit east of the four stars called the Water Jar of Aquarius, and Saturn will be about a block to the right.

The fact is the Water Jar of Aquarius looks about as much like a water jar as Pegasus looks like a flying horse. Nor does Aquarius as a whole or in part resemble any water-bearer I ever met, though there is a general sprinkling effect. Aquarius, you know, is supposed to be pouring water into Formalhaut, the mouth of Pisces Austrinus, the Southern Fish, if you see any sense in that.

Personally, I get a kick out of Saturn's nine moons, the ninth and smallest of which is named Phoebe. Some say Phoebe is only forty miles in diameter. She revolves around Saturn in a direction contrary to that of the other eight moons, and they can't do a thing about it. If you ask me, she'll continue to do so. She's different, that's all.

September 6

THE Pilgrim Fathers sailed from Plymouth, England, for America on the *Mayflower* on September 6, 1620, making this something of an anniversary. What's more, the *Mayflower* was about ninety feet long and twenty-four feet wide, and its 102 passengers included forty-four grown men, nineteen grown women, twenty-nine young men and boys, and ten young women and girls. The prettiest passenger, so far as I am concerned, was Priscilla Mullins.

Longfellow calls Priscilla the loveliest maiden of Plymouth. We see eye to eye on that, anyway. But he was wrong about Priscilla's riding home on a snow-white bull after her marriage to John Alden. She couldn't have ridden on a bull of any color because there were no cattle of any kind in Plymouth then, let alone a snow-white bull. Priscilla and John were married late in 1622 or early in 1623. Edward Winslow brought the first bull and the first heifers to Plymouth when he returned from England in 1624, and it is my impression that the bull was not white. We might as well get these things straight.

September 7

THIS is Queen Elizabeth's birthday, and I'd say it rates honorable mention. Elizabeth arrived at Greenwich Palace on Sunday afternoon, September 7, 1533, much to the disappointment of Henry VIII and Anne Boleyn, who wanted a boy. Henry beheaded Anne a couple of years later, but not for that reason—it was just his way.

Queen Elizabeth didn't mind getting birthday presents at all. If she didn't get plenty she would hint. A Mrs. Carre once gave her a sheet of fine cambric embroidered in many colors with birds, beasts, and serpents. I know how she felt for I recently received as a birthday gift a framed exhibit consisting of blue seashells, some purple grass, a small defunct craft, what appears to be several green feathers, and a clamshell labeled "Atlantic City, New Jersey."

If Elizabeth felt that she hadn't received enough presents, she was inclined to take whatever appealed to her. She was a delightful guest, but you had to watch your spoons.

September 8

IF YOU have nothing else to do, you might divide your Hardy Phlox, if they need it.

Some of our birds are departing for the south already, so maybe we can all get a little sleep. New England asters are at their peak, and the mackerel are running again.

Artichokes are plentiful now, but a lot of husbands won't eat them. How about meat loaf?

Of course, lemon meringue pie, cinnamon buns, and devil's food cake are good any time. And don't forget pickled onions!

As for me, I'll stick to hamburger.

September 9

AND that reminds me that Luigi Galvani, a headliner in electrical science, was born at Bologna, Italy, on September 9, 1737. He's the one who noticed a twitching in the leg of a frog when he accidently touched it with a scalpel which had been lying near an electrical machine of some kind. If I remember correctly, he was making some frog broth for his wife at the time. Some people will eat anything.

Right then and there, it seems, Professor Galvani got up his famous theory of animal electricity, which turned out to be all wrong in its essential features, especially the part about the frog.

Galvani was mistaken about the amount of electricity in frogs, but he had some good ideas, too, for the galvanometer is named in his honor, and you don't have galvanometers named after you merely for making a mistake about a frog. He was regarded as a whiz at the University of Bologna. And he is still known wherever galvanometers are known.

September 10

WELL, why beat about the bush? Today's hero of history is Commodore Oliver Hazard Perry, who won the Battle of Lake Erie on September 10, 1813.

I'm afraid I've been thinking of Commodore Oliver Hazard Perry as the man who made the treaty with Japan, when all the time it was Commodore Matthew Calbraith Perry, his younger brother. I don't pretend to be a shark on early American history, but I may say that Matthew Calbraith Perry comes as something of a surprise at this late date. Now I don't know what to believe.

September 11

ON SEPTEMBER 11, 1609, Henry Hudson sailed into New York Harbor on the *Half Moon* and got his first glimpse of the Hudson River, discovered eighty-five years before by Giovanni da Verrazano. He thought it might be the Northwest Passage, a short cut to Asia, which everybody had been trying to find

for a long time. So he sailed up the river, hoping to land in China or Japan any minute.

It looked like success between Yonkers and Peekskill, but it was all off by the time they reached Albany, where the water was only a few feet deep. Hudson sent a small boat as far as Troy, but it was no use.

On his way back to the ocean he saw a place full of Indians called Mannahattes and this soon resulted in Peter Minuit and Wouter Van Twiller and that sort of thing. Peter Minuit bought Manhattan Island with his $24 and Wouter Van Twiller bought Governors Island, which was then known as Nut Island, because it contained more nuts than Manhattan. That was three hundred years ago.

Hudson named his river the Great River of the Mountains, and the Dutch settlers named it the North River to distinguish it from the South River, wherever that is. Today we call it the

Hudson River, although some people call it the North River to distinguish it from the East River.

Hudson's Strait and Hudson's Bay weren't really discovered by Henry Hudson, either. On the second of his four voyages, however, he saw a mermaid. Or, rather, two members of his crew saw her. So something came of that trip.

September 12

I'VE never been one to have the young of the more prominent carnivora roaming about in my house, like some people. Nor do I pal with persons who go in heavily for lion, tiger, and bear cubs, cute as these little animals may be. One doesn't mind so much their scratching and clawing until one's exposed parts bear a close resemblance to hamburger, but there comes a time when these babies suddenly grow up, and for all I know the change could occur overnight. Watch out, say the experts, when lion or tiger cubs start eating raw meat. Once they have taken a good big hunk out of their owner, they may be said to have reached that stage.

"Never make a pet of a bear," a zoo keeper once warned me, with what struck me as needless alarm.

I may make wrong moves from time to time, but I have never come even close to making a pet of a bear.

September 13

"DEAR SIR: I am about to give my first small dinner. Do you think eggplant would be a safe bet?

"Uneasy"

It's a good thing you didn't invite me. I don't mean to upset you, *Uneasy*, but eggplant leaves me cold. And there must be other people on this earth who feel the same way.

Of course to some people eggplant always tastes like something else. You could have a little guessing game built around the eggplant, and the party might turn into a howling social success. You never can tell.

I'd trust to luck, and serve up plenty of the main dish just in case.

September 14

MAYBE it's not front-page news, but this is the birthday of Friedrich Heinrich Alexander von Humboldt, eminent naturalist and traveler, who started life in Berlin on September 14, 1769. I don't think very much of his famous saying, "I despise mankind in all its strata."

Naturally, Humboldt was grouchy at times, with all he had on his mind. He was the leading authority on most of the sciences, and he invented more. He had to measure all the mountains and volcanoes he could find, too—I forget why. While measuring Mount Chimborazo, he found a fly at an altitude of 16,600 feet. Before that flies had never been found above 15,000 feet.

Humboldt also had a pet chameleon, whose strange antics he used to observe. I can see how that might get awfully tiresome, but would it cause one to despise mankind in all its strata? It may have been something he ate.

September 15

"DEAR SIR: Where do you stand on the founding of a National Eat More Parsnips Week? Are you with us or against us?

"Parsnip Lover"

I haven't anything in particular against the parsnip, excepting that, if memory serves, I'd just as soon have something else. It's been quite a while since I've had one.

Still, I don't want you to think that I'm stubborn about parsnips. So many people have hated them that there must be a lot of good in them. I once knew a girl—otherwise very wonderful—who made parsnip soup, parsnip salad, parsnip patties, parsnip muffins, parsnip chowder, parsnip croquettes—also parsnips baked, boiled, creamed, escalloped, fried, and mashed, as well as parsnip dumpling pot pie. It was the parsnip dumpling pot pie that got me.

Parsnips may be just what some people need. They certainly need *something*.

September 16

JACOPO ROBUSTI, famous Italian painter, was born in Venice on September 16, 1518. His father was a dyer, so Jacopo was nicknamed Tintoretto, or Little Dyer. He was a pupil of Titian, who said he would never amount to a hill of beans. Titian was wrong, for Tintoretto's paintings are now worth a lot of money. Titian is remembered chiefly for his hair.

Tintoretto's output in actual square feet was ten times as large as Titian's. His largest painting, *Paradise*, measures 75 x 30 feet and contains 500 figures. Well, show me a bigger one!

I might say more about Tintoretto, but I wouldn't come by it honestly. I was brought up on the Barbizon School myself, for our house was a hotbed of reproductions of pictures by Jean François Millet, perhaps the outstanding artist of the Passepartout Age. You're probably too young to know about passepartout, a method of framing anything you could get your hands on with tape and hanging it on the wall. If you ran into a sale of Jean François Millet's works, so much the better.

And was it fun? I really can't say at this distance. We thought it was fun at the time.

Our Millet stand-bys were *The Gleaners, The Angelus,* and *The Man With a Hoe,* all of which made nice presents to people who already had several copies of each.

September 17

"DEAR SIR: What is the origin of the term *literary lion?*
"Ambitious"

It seems that the kings of England used to keep a number of lions in the Tower of London, for want of something better to do, and these animals were the first thing visitors to the city always went to see, because as soon as they got home somebody would be sure to ask them: "Did you see the lions?" Persons who answered this question in the negative were regarded as nobody much. Gradually the Tower beasts got to be an old story, and the expression *the lions* was applied to any other object of strange and unusual appearance which one mustn't miss, such as two-headed calves and—well, this is getting a bit delicate, but you see how it happened.

September 18

DOCTOR Samuel Johnson, who wrote a dictionary, was born at Litchfield, Staffordshire, England, on September 18, 1709. Of course you've heard of the man who said the dictionary was a very interesting book but it didn't seem to have much of a plot. Well, a friend of mine says the trouble with the dictionary is that you have to know how a word is spelled before you can look it up to see how it is spelled. Sometimes I think there's a weak link in his argument, if one could only find it. At other times I think he may have hit upon a self-evident truth.

September 19

WE HEAR a lot about ragweed these days, but who ever mentions camel dander? We all know that ragweed causes hay fever in persons sensitive to its pollen and that such persons will go on sneezing until frost. Well, camel dander causes sneezing, too, and it lasts the year round. I'd call it a menace.

If camel dander makes you sneeze, you have camel fever, or camel asthma. If you are constantly sneezing, with maybe a touch of dermatitis and other scattering symptoms, you ought to investigate camel asthma before you go blaming ragweed for all your troubles.

Victims of camel dander have several moves. You can keep away from camels, thus avoiding the animal's dander, or epithelium, which flies around in the air much as pollen does and with far less reason. Or you can select camels with the least possible amount of epithelium.

You might even take up giraffes instead. Giraffes only kick you and knock you down. Camels bite, but they come cheaper than giraffes. I'm afraid you'll have to decide for yourself.

September 20

PEOPLE who sneer at the herring simply don't know their fish. Herrings come of a very old family, fossil herrings having been found in the Eocene rocks of Wyoming. Few fish can say the same. It is practically certain that herrings, or something closely resembling them, were the original parents of all the fish of today, and you can like it or not.

Nobody really knows why herrings suddenly leave one place for another. It probably seems like a good idea at the time. Or they may feel that travel is broadening.

I started to say that large schools of herrings will enter our inlets to spawn any day now. I'm taking it pretty calmly myself.

September 21

WHERE would we be today if John Loudon McAdam hadn't been born in Ayr, Scotland, on September 21, 1756? We would have no macadam roads, that's what! We might have macsweeney roads or macsmithized roads, but things wouldn't be the same.

Mr. McAdam began to macadamize roads in Scotland in 1783, after he had lived in New York for a while and made a fortune, as people did in those days. He bought an estate at Sauhrie, Ayrshire, and started filling roads with pieces of broken stone, and nobody could stop him. There were so many complaints that the government became interested and gave him authority to place broken stone on the roads without let or hindrance.

Before he died, in 1836, Mr. McAdam had macadamized most of the roads in the British Isles. He held that each successive layer of broken stone should be ground down by the wheels of carriages and wagons passing over it in the ordinary way of business and pleasure, and by no other method. You see how that would work out.

The carriages and wagons would finally grind down the stones, however, so that people could ride on them without jolting themselves silly, and the nervous wrecks would begin to chirk up. Then Mr. McAdam would put on another layer of stone.

Macadam roads have now been greatly improved. Today we have concrete, tar, asphalt, and what not on our roads, and the jolting is done by machinery. So far as I know, there was no Mr. Asphalt.

September 22

"DEAR SIR: My boy friend has many good qualities, but he seems to have an ugly temper. What shall I do?
"*Desperate*"

Take a little dry starch, moisten it with cold water, and apply to the injured part. Do this at once, to prevent the air from touching the area. No discoloration should result.

Some authorities recommend raw beefsteak.

September 23

WHAT with the influence of elementary education upon the growing mind, it is not too much to say that McGuffey's Eclectic Readers explain why millions of American citizens are the way they are. This is a good day to say it because William Holmes McGuffey, author and compiler, was born in Washington County, Pennsylvania, on September 23, 1800.

As some one has put it, Mr. McGuffey taught the moral and intellectual virtues of integrity, honesty, industry, temperance, true patriotism, courage, politeness, and then some. He not only taught them, he rubbed them in.

Perhaps I was considered too backward for the First Reader, for I had a Primer, in which there was a cat and a rat. Ann was there, too, and the rat ran at Ann and the cat ran at the rat. Then Nat arrived, and the rat ran at Nat. Nat had a fat dog named Rab, who saw a frog on a log. So Rab ran at the frog for a change.

A very strange thing happened to Ann and Nat in Lesson VIII, where they suddenly grew up, as you could see by the picture. It seems that Ann had a mat and Nat had a lamp.

They had pooled their resources for the evening, because the lamp is on the mat, all lighted up, right between Ann and Nat. Nat must have brought the lamp with him when he came to call.

Next day, though, Ann and Nat were themselves again. Nat was on Tom's nag and Ann was on the log, where the frog had been. The rat was still at large.

September 24

STRANGE what will ruin one's day. I always thought Zachary Taylor, our twelfth President, invented the wisecrack, "Trust in God and keep your powder dry." It struck me as a pretty cute remark, though I've heard a lot better.

Now it turns out that Oliver Cromwell said it first. I hope I'm not prejudiced, but nothing that old kill-joy could say would be any good. It seems that once when Cromwell's soldiers were about to cross a stream, he yelled, "Put your trust in God, but mind to keep your powder dry." In the first place, there are too many words in that for a good slogan. And the grammar looks a little shaky to me.

There is no authority for calling Cromwell Old Mealy-Mouth, but the phrase certainly fits him. Zachary Taylor was called Old Zach and Old Rough and Ready, and also Old Buena Vista for defeating the Mexicans, probably at Buena Vista. General Winfield Scott, another hero of the Mexican War, was called Old Fuss and Feathers, but he never became President.

By the way, Zachary Taylor was born in Orange County, Virginia, on September 24, 1784.

September 25

"DEAR SIR: Please explain the origin of the English slang expression, 'What a shocking bad hat!'

"Puzzled"

It won't do you a bit of good, but it seems there was an eminent hatter running for office in Southwark (pronounced *Sutherk*), a borough of London, who tried to win votes by stopping citizens on the street and exclaiming, "What a shocking bad hat you have got! Call at my warehouse and you shall have a new one!" This struck many persons as a fine idea, so they went around crying, "What a shocking bad hat!" until that was about all you could hear in London. It is my impression that the hatter was defeated at the polls.

In order to forestall further letters of this sort, I may add that I don't know any more inside stuff about Early Victorian slang, such as "Has your mother sold her mangle?" "Hookey Walker!" and "There she goes with her eye out!" All these expressions are rapidly dying out and are now seldom used except by certain fine old county families which have not heard about recent changes in this and that.

September 26

YOU'LL have trouble finding a lower form of lizard than the skink. A few of the species are quite limbless. Perhaps we do not experiment enough with skinks, but there is so much else to do.

If you drop a skink onto the sand it will instantly disappear underground. And good riddance.

September 27

"DEAR SIR: What is a Barmecide Feast and where can I get one?

"*Gourmet*"

You mean you actually don't know that a Barmecide Feast is an imaginary meal composed of imaginary food? It seems the Barmecides were a family of Persian princes in the time of Haroun-al-Raschid. And one day, when a beggar asked one of the Barmecides for something to eat the Barmecide thought he would play a little joke. So he pretended to serve up a wonderful banquet, but all the dishes and glasses were empty. Well, the beggar played the game for a while, then he pretended to get very drunk on the imaginary wine and gave the Barmecide a sock in the eye which knocked him cold. And that is what comes of trying to be funny at the wrong time.

September 28

ON THIS date in 1929 four Navajo Indians, after drinking eleven quarts of something or other, tried to burn their bootlegger at the stake near Flagstaff, Arizona, and were fined thirty dollars each. Colonel and Mrs. Charles A. Lindbergh, Jr., stopped off at Baranquilla, Colombia, for a few hours. President Herbert Hoover, Mrs. Hoover, Herbert Hoover, Jr., and guests arrived at the Hoover fishing camp in the Blue Ridge Mountains. Mrs. Dolly Gann was temporarily in Topeka, but was expected back in Washington in time for the visit of Prime Minister J. Ramsay MacDonald of Great Britain the following week. And Frank Turco of Glasco, New York, was bitten by a hog which he was driving to market in an automobile. The hog was in a crate but managed it somehow.

September 29

WELL, the fly-swatting season is almost over for this year—
just as it was getting good, naturally. It is now time to look
back and see what one has accomplished during the summer.

I think I may say my own technique showed a definite
improvement. I also made some progress in the psychology of
the fly. A fly will not settle while you're looking at him, or at
any rate, while *I* am looking at him. I don't claim any credit
for this; it's just a fact.

This year I developed a sort of oblique approach. I pretend
to be hugely interested in something else altogether, thus
throwing my victims off their guard. But all the time I'm

watching out of the corner of my eye, or of both eyes, if necessary. At the proper instant, I pounce.

The time I've spent trying to seem casual with flies has not been wasted, although looking obliquely at several flies at once is terribly hard on the eyes, involving as it does an almost complete break with the laws of vision. Maybe a better system could be worked out by some energetic young man or woman with a good backhand. There's no harm in trying.

September 30

IF YOU were born between September 24 and October 23 you are under the Sign of Libra, or the Scales. Libra persons promote justice and harmony in the home, especially when they get their own way. Libra is full of actresses and Presidents of the United States, and other public-spirited citizens, including Alice Joyce, Eleanora Duse, Sarah Bernhardt, Helen Hayes, Zachary Taylor, Rutherford Burchard Hayes, Chester Alan Arthur, and Frances E. Willard. Some Libra persons are just a wee bit different from other Libra persons, such as Oscar Wilde, Jonathan Edwards, Lily Langtry, Edith Cavell, James Whitcomb Riley, Friedrich Wilhelm Nietzsche, Giuseppe Verdi, J. Ramsay MacDonald, Edward W. Bok, Wilton Lackaye, John L. Sullivan, Saint Francis, Oom Paul Kruger, William Penn, William Wrigley, Jr., John Dewey, Fannie Hurst, and Jenny Lind.

OCTOBER

October 1

WELL, here it is October already. October is so named because it was the eighth month in the old Roman year and *octo,* or something of the sort, means eight. It's the tenth month in our year, so the name sounds rather foolish if you've gone to the trouble of looking it up in the encyclopedia. We could change the name of October to December, which means the tenth month (according to the old Romans), but there wouldn't be much sense in that, either. The Anglo-Saxons called the month Winterfylleth, which is even worse. All in all, perhaps we'd better let it alone. A great many people believe that October means the Month of the Leaf-Falling Moons, and it would be a shame to shatter their illusions.

October 2

"DEAR SIR: Where can I find the rest of the poem beginning, 'If 'twere done when 'twere done, 'twere done'? I have always wondered how it turned out.

"Worried"

You doubtless allude to the passage in *Macbeth* (Act I, Scene 7) where Macbeth, or possibly Lady Macbeth, is discussing the murder of King Duncan or Banquo's Ghost or the Three Witches or some such thing. Anyway, one of them remarks:

If it were done when 'tis done, then 'twere well
It were done quickly.

Unfortunately, Bartlett's Quotations doesn't say what happened next. The speech means that if it *were* done when it *is* done—I'm sure you can manage from there on. But on the whole I prefer your version. There's something about it.

October 3

AN EMINENT literary critic says that he never trusts people who can't punctuate. He says there must be something fundamentally wrong with the brains of such people. I resent that. I have always thought that punctuation must be taught in the eighth grade, which I was allowed to skip because I was so good in geography in the seventh grade. It wouldn't surprise me to learn that a certain critic has spent *two* years in the eighth grade. At least he's very free with his commas. He could always get a job in a newspaper proof room as a comma-putter-in. He is also very confident about his *shalls* and *wills*. I think they taught that in the eighth grade, too.

October 4

"DEAR SIR: I have been feeling pretty nervous about things in general, and my doctor has ordered me not to worry. What do you advise?

"*Bridge-Crosser*"

If I were you I would send the doctor a little statement of my financial condition, and maybe he will settle with the telephone, electric, gas, and installment people. He probably intended to do that all along, or he would hardly have given you such a prescription. Or he may be planning to send you a nice big check as a surprise. Doctors are really fine fellows, if you give them half a chance.

I don't want to influence you, but why *not* worry? Personally, I worry a little every day. I intend to keep right on doing so and I should like to see any doctor try to stop me. As for nervousness, what do you think your nerves are for, anyway? I also make a point of being nervous whenever I feel good and like it. It seems to rest me.

October 5

ON OCTOBER 5, 1860, Henry Thoreau saw a fish hawk skimming over Walden Pond. It caught several fish and then flew away. Three days later he saw two strange woodpeckers sitting in a pine tree. They had white throats and yellow spots at the base of the upper mandible. He thought they might be Arctic Three-Toed Woodpeckers. Most of Thoreau's biographers now believe that they probably *were* Arctic Three-Toed Woodpeckers, but they say that the yellow spots must have been on the top of the head because that is where Arctic Three-Toed Woodpeckers have yellow spots. I have often won-

dered what life would be like if one were just terribly interested in Arctic Three-Toed Woodpeckers. It might be worth
trying.

October 6

ON THIS date in 1927 Miss Mercedes Gleitze, a London
typist, swam the English Channel on her eighth attempt.
Large numbers of trout, seeking the headwaters of the Salmon
River, were halted by a new concrete dam at Malone, New
York. Local fish lovers netted hundreds of the trout, carried
them above the dam, and turned them loose, and everybody
was happy. Professor Dudley Joy Morton of the Yale Medical

School announced that human beings probably began to separate themselves from the other primate stocks about 10,000,000 years ago. He said it was 2,000,000 years more before you could see much difference. Science has made up its mind, but popular opinion varies about whether we came from monkeys or something of the sort. To me it seems perfectly clear that some of us did and some of us didn't.

October 7

"DEAR SIR: Can't you do something about noise abatement?
"Frantic"

If you mean can't I have a law passed making noise illegal, I'm afraid the answer is no. And if I could, nothing would come of it, *Frantic*, because people as a whole like noise and are going to have it or know the reason why. In my opinion, those who dislike noise will have to muddle along without the aid of new laws or constitutional amendments—it's a case of every man for himself. Have you tried stuffing your fingers in your ears? Personally, I'm taking the matter up with a couple of darling old ladies whose windows adjoin mine. For several years now they have been discussing something having to do with their Aunt Josephine, starting promptly at seven o'clock each morning. I'm going to ask them how they would like to keep their traps shut.

October 8

ON THIS date in 1871, at nine o'clock in the evening, Mrs. O'Leary's cow kicked over a lamp and started the Great Chicago Fire, which caused a property damage of $196,000,000 and left 98,860 Chicagoans homeless. Some say the cow was named Bessie, some say Maud. And some, including the members of the O'Leary family, say there was no such cow at all. I regard this as a dangerous tendency. If Mrs. O'Leary's cow did not kick over that lamp, what *can* we be sure of? Personally, I was taught that she did. She has now become a part of my general outlook and I'd find it pretty hard to change. I can see the O'Learys' side of it, but what about me?

October 9

"DEAR SIR: I am giving a dinner for eight persons and should like to do the thing right. I wonder if you would part with one of your famous recipes for the occasion. You seem to know everything.

"Admirer"

You have evidently confused me with my Granduncle Jasper, who mixed his own salad dressing in season and out. We never speak of him any more. Maybe you'd be interested in a swell dessert we children used to wangle in the old days, called Paperhanger's Delight. You just sprinkle a little flour in boiling water, stir gently, and there you are. A dash of nutmeg on top does wonders. The beauty of this dessert is that you can really use it for wallpaper. In that way you save the nutmeg.

October 10

IT'S just as well to remember these days that poison ivy is the three-leaved kind. Right now it has turned to a lovely shade of red for reasons which doubtless strike it as perfectly adequate, however mistaken they may seem from some points of view. The beauty of poison ivy in October is probably one of Mother Nature's devices for getting even with some people. When discussing poison ivy with a stranger, never say that you'd think a lot of low-grade morons would go out and pick a big bouquet of it and take it home, because it always turns out that he did that very thing himself only last autumn. Maybe you did, too, but that's different.

October 11

NOW that the evenings are drawing in, and current literature being what it is, one may derive a mild satisfaction from reading the encyclopedia. I haven't got far with it yet, but I have already learned a number of interesting things about the letter A. It seems that among the Phoenicians the letter A—well, I don't remember exactly what it was, but the information is there any time I want it. It won't be long now until I get to Aa and Aabenraa. I've peeked ahead and discovered that Aa is the name of many small European rivers. Personally, I'm not crazy about having so many rivers named Aa. Life seems hard enough without that.

October 12

SEEMS too bad America didn't get named after Christopher Columbus who discovered us on this date in 1492. Or, rather, he discovered some nearby islands, and it came to the same thing in the long run. The worst of it is that we were named by a certain Professor Waldseemüller, who got all mixed up in his facts and thought the credit belonged to Amerigo Vespucci, which it didn't at all. So Professor Waldseemüller gave the name of America to the New World in a geography that he published in 1507, and from that day to this nobody has ever had time to fix it. Isn't that the way things go in this world?

October 13

YOU'VE probably never thought about it much before, but the hippopotamus can walk along the bottom of a river with great rapidity.

The bones of a small hippo were discovered on the island of Cyprus, and those of a tiny elephant on Malta. This has led to the theory that the smaller the country the smaller the animal—that the size of an animal depends on the size of the territory he inhabits.

An interesting theory, but where docs it leave the Kodiak (Island) Bear, an enormous fellow? Or, for that matter, the tiny Koala Bear of Australia?

I'm only asking.

October 14

"DEAR SIR: Is it true that fish are good for the brain, or is that only a rumor?

"Worried"

You have raised a rather complicated question, *Worried*. Whether a diet of fish improves the brain depends partly upon the fish used and partly upon the brain involved. Some people could eat fish from now till Doomsday and be little the wiser. The Trobriand Islanders, for instance, live almost entirely upon fish and they can't even speak English. If you are trying a fish diet for your intellect, maybe you'd better take a few other steps, too, just to be on the safe side—the fish can't do it all! Why not do some good reading and build up your basal metabolism? Then, if nothing happens, don't blame the fish.

October 15

WELL, the muskrats are building their houses already, so maybe we're in for a hard winter. If they build earlier than usual, you know, the season will be severe. Unfortunately, I don't know whether this is especially early and I couldn't swear that the muskrats I saw were actually building houses. But they were swimming around and carrying things in their mouths and I was told they were muskrats. It would probably be more scientific to watch the squirrels and see if they are storing up more nuts this year, but who knows how many nuts they stored *last* year? I'm waiting to hear from the goose-bone prophets, who are likely to report any day now. I'll string along with them.

October 16

THIS is Noah Webster's birthday. No, not Daniel—*Noah*. Noah Webster was born October 16, 1758, at West Hartford, Connecticut, and was not, as I had always believed until a few minutes ago, a brother of Daniel's. Daniel was a much more emotional type, rather given to flowery quotations, such as "Sink or swim, live or die, survive or perish, I give my hand and my heart to this vote." Noah would mull over his learned books for hours in absolute silence and then startle everybody by remarking: "The Zarp is a species of Zimp indigenous to Madagascar and Eastern Abyssinia." His dictionary was published in 1828 and is still going strong in a bigger and better edition. Of Noah's great work, some of us can say, with an elderly friend of a friend of mine: "I've hefted it and I respect it, but I ain't read it."

October 17

ON OCTOBER 17, 1777, Gentleman Johnny Burgoyne surrendered to General Gates at Saratoga, which was the ruination of Gentleman Johnny and the beginning of the end of the Revolution. It wasn't entirely his fault, for General Howe, who was expected to effect a junction with him at Albany,

went to Philadelphia instead, and that is no way to effect a junction at Albany. General Howe had a good excuse, too, because Lord George Germain never sent his instructions. Lord George was spending the week end in Sussex and couldn't wait five minutes to sign them, and then he forgot all about it. Gentleman Johnny was also called Handsome Jack. In a painting of his surrender at Saratoga he looks as though he had won the war and would do it again as often as it should become necessary. He always looked like that.

October 18

NOBODY seems to know who gave the name of Indian Summer to those warm, balmy days we generally get somewhere along in the autumn after the first threat of winter. It may have been someone who had heard that Nanibozhu, a deity of the Ojibways, always sits down beside the North Pole and smokes his pipe for a while before falling asleep for the winter. But for me that doesn't solve the problem—it only raises a lot of other problems. Some say that Indian Summer is merely a couple of words from the Choctaw, meaning Indian Summer. Others say it's just one of those expressions that we were all brought up on.

October 19

SOME people like parsnips at any time, but October has been called the Parsnip Month, probably by someone who was trying to be funny. You'll see parsnips all over the market these days and, what is more surprising, you'll see people buying them. Parsnips have the rather moderate fuel value of 294 calories per pound. Wouldn't you think that anything containing so much wood-fiber would make better fuel? I prefer my wood-fiber straight, but you come across lots of people who crave it in the form of parsnips. O. O. McIntyre thought that parsnips, when properly prepared, are among our finest vegetables. Mr. McIntyre hated beets, though, but who doesn't? Of course, parsnips belong to the family Umbelliferae, but that only means that they have umbels. A *carrot* can have umbels!

"DEAR SIR: How do cross-word puzzles affect the mind and what is a six-letter Chinese wombat beginning with z?

"Toots"

If you will just relax and read your question over again, you may get an inkling about the mental hazards involved—it practically answers itself. As for the Chinese wombat, what makes you think it begins with a z? You have probably misspelled some other word, thus getting a z where no z exists, or you may have read the directions too hastily. Are you sure the word isn't *zareba*, a hedge or palisade protecting a camp or village in the Soudan? I'm afraid there are no zarebas in China, but there are certainly no wombats there, either. Better start all over, *Toots*, just to make sure.

I was going to be a bit severe with you and your puzzles, but you've got me doing them again, after all these years. And what do you think is a four-letter word for leavings, beginning with *o*? Well, it's *orts*, from the Old Friesic. An ort is a morsel of food left from a meal, but it is seldom used in the singular—one generally says *orts* if one says it at all.

And by the way, what has become of our old friend the emu, an Australian bird allied to the cassowary? There are a lot of new animals now, including a South American rodent called the paca, and also the onoa, or wild ox of Celebes, but they will never take the place of the emu. I don't like this scarcity of emus—is it a sign of the times, or what?

October 21

IF YOU love snakes, go ahead and keep a garter snake and see if I care. I might add that some supposedly innocent snakes do quite a bit of constricting, by and large. None of our native snakes, however, is strong enough to hurt you in that way unless he concentrates on your neck.

For instance, if your bull snake is a large one, you shouldn't allow him to get more than a coil or two around your neck, and you must be sure where his head and tail are all the time, since you may need them to pry him off.

Grabbing madly at the coils and screaming won't help a bit. It only makes things worse.

October 22

IF IT'S clear tonight, do me a favor and look straight up at the sky about eight o'clock. You'll see a big yellowish star, but that isn't the one—that's Deneb. The much brighter bluish star about two blocks west is Vega, our fourth brightest star. Vega is a star with a future, for in about 12,000 years it will be the polestar because of the Precession of the Equinoxes—which you'd better just take for granted unless you're very, very good at such things. Vega is rather close to us, as stars go, being only twenty-six light years distant. One light year is 186,284 times 31,536,000 miles, so it counts up—Rigel, the second best star in Orion, is 540 light years away, if you believe all you hear. I forget why I went into all this, but Vega is worth knowing anyhow. It may come to me later.

October 23

LOOK out for frost these late October nights. Very few people understand frost. The frost experts understand it, but they can't explain it very clearly to the likes of us—it's a good thing we know frost when we see it. The rule is that the more an expert knows about frost the worse he is at explaining. According to frostologists, frost is not frozen dew, because frozen dew would be little balls of ice instead of frost. Frost forms when the dew point is below 32 degrees Fahrenheit. The temperature at which condensation of moisture takes place, whether it is going to be rain, hail, or whatever, is called the dew point. Isn't that cute? Some day we must take up dew in real earnest. By the way, frost has been found very useful in wearing down mountains and converting the rocks into soil, so if you want any mountains worn down you know what to do.

October 24

ASTROLOGICALLY speaking, persons born between October 24 and November 22 are under the Sign of Scorpio—but it's not as bad as it sounds. Some Scorpio persons will sting you if they get the chance and others are perfect darlings. Eminent Scorpians include Ignace Jan Paderewski, John Philip Sousa, Jackie Coogan, Martin Luther, Samuel Insull, Lord Macaulay, Will Rogers, Benvenuto Cellini, Billy Sunday, President Theodore Roosevelt, Eugene V. Debs, Edwin Booth, Owen D. Young, President Warren Gamaliel Harding, William Cullen Bryant, and Daniel Boone. On the distaff side are Maude Adams, Marie Antoinette, Ida M. Tarbell, George Eliot, St. Cecilia, and Hetty Green. Scorpio persons seldom take lemon in their tea, and prefer two lumps of sugar.

October 25

ON THIS date in 1929 a Rhode Island Red hen belonging to David Williams, of Lake Titus, New York, adopted five kittens she found meowing in a barn. The Senate of the

United States adopted a tariff rate of 5½ cents per pound on casein, and President Herbert Hoover and guests returned to Washington from a four-day trip to Detroit and the Ohio River country. And—oh, yes! The stock market seemed to be acting strangely, but President Hoover said not to worry.

I have never understood what happened. An acquaintance of mine lost his last cent, and then he lost his last cent several times afterwards, and kept on that way for years. Every time he lost his last cent he would go to Palm Beach for a week or sell another apartment building. How do people manage those things?

October 26

"DEAR SIR: I have trouble in introducing groups of people to one another, especially when there are about three groups. As I am giving a rather large party soon I want this cleared up a little. Can you suggest something?

"Constant Reader"

I suggest leaving for parts unknown. If you persist in giving this party it can only end in the same old feeling that you have made a show of yourself again. In spite of anything you can do at this late date, most of the guests will go around saying that you were evidently brought up in a barn. Introducing groups, my friend, is a lifework, and you must decide now whether you wish to devote yourself henceforth to this one cause. There are people who do it perfectly, but I have noticed that they generally leave something to be desired in other directions.

When I am caught between groups I find it·a good plan to yell "Fire!" and escape during the excitement.

October 27

TODAY our reptiles are satisfied with crawling along the ground and climbing an occasional tree, but in the old days—before the invention of the airplane—reptiles flew.

The Pterodactyl couldn't possibly have been classified as a bird, because birds are warm-blooded. Of course, modern bats are warm-blooded, too, but that doesn't make them birds. Like whales, bats are mammals. There's one thing you can say for a bat—it's not a reptile.

Twentieth-century bats think they invented their method of flying. They are not aware that Pterodactyls beat them to it.

Bats are on the way out. Everybody knows it except the bats themselves.

October 28

I WONDER if I've ever told you what I've been through trying to make chipped beef gravy. It's an infantile fixation, I guess—my craving. My mother used to make it but I've given up all hope of achieving anything like that. Mother's was a darkish kind—a brownish color; all I ever come up with is pale.

It seems you make a white sauce and put in the chipped beef. The white sauce is what's thrown me—lumps, you know. You put in butter, then flour, and then milk, adding it slowly, and it turns out to be full of lumps.

In desperation, I tried mixing it in a bowl first, then transferring the result into the frying pan. Instead of finishing in the original lumps, the flour etcetera seems to spread out and sort of concentrate into what resembles a layer of very thick blotting paper.

This amorphous substance breaks apart into small pieces, looking vaguely like dumpling material. But to say that it can

be stirred up into the gravy so as to be unnoticeable is just untrue. It does not tend to disintegrate in the least.

Maybe I worry too much about the little things of life. Still, if one wants chipped beef gravy one doesn't want tapioca pudding, and one certainly doesn't want a low form of dumpling. One wants chipped beef gravy, and if there's any justice there ought to be some way of getting it.

October 29

ON THIS date in 1618 Sir Walter Raleigh was beheaded for conspiring against James I of England, a king who is famous for spilling soup on his vest and never washing his face. If Queen Elizabeth had lived, Sir Walter might not have been beheaded. Some historians say that Sir Walter never threw his plush cape into a puddle for Queen Elizabeth to step on. He did so!

October 30

BECAUSE I once mentioned a star—Vega, I think it was—I am asked to announce that Orion is now at its best. All right, consider it announced. I'm glad to do this, although my own feeling is that Orion doesn't need the publicity and that it doesn't give a hoot whether it is looked at or not. Orion is our most spectacular winter constellation and is now to be seen high up in the southern sky at a reasonable time each evening —say around eleven o'clock. To some people Orion looks like a giant hunter with a belt of three diagonal stars and lion's skin on his left arm. To others it looks just like any other mess of stars. Betelgeuse, Orion's best star, is said to be twenty-seven million times as large as our sun—a figure which I, personally, accept with a grain of salt. Be that as it may, I still feel that Orion can take care of itself.

"DEAR SIR: What is ducking for apples, and how does one go about it? It sounds frightfully amusing.

"Pro Bono Publico"

Now, that's a coincidence, because I was just about to say that ducking for apples is a popular Hallowe'en sport in Great Britain and other places where the old customs are observed, especially if they are a bit whimsical. It is a relic of pagan times—in fact, it is named after the old pagan ceremony of ducking for apples. One doesn't generally think of pagans in that way, but they seem to have been just kids at heart when they weren't up to something worse. Anyway, you fill a tub with water, add the apples, and have the children try to catch the apples with their teeth. As this practically cannot be done, it affords no little entertainment to a certain kind of grown-up and a great deal of water on the best rug. The modern child is not very antiquarian in its tastes, so maybe you'd better forget it.

NOVEMBER

November 1

NOVEMBER is a rather trying month in some respects. The Anglo-Saxons called it Windmonath, or Wind Month, for obvious reasons. The Anglo-Saxons were unobservant in many ways, but they could tell when the wind blew—give them credit for that. What the Jutes called November is unknown. I have often wondered what the Jutes thought about things in general, but the more one wonders the more complicated it becomes. Before one could make any headway with this problem it would be necessary to determine what a Jute actually was, and that is no laughing matter. Nowadays November is often called the Month of Blue Devils, because everybody is a little gloomy over the passing of summer. Some people just call it November and let it go at that.

November 2

ANY little boy born today may become President of the United States if he always eats his spinach and stays in good with the right people. James Knox Polk, our eleventh President, was born November 2, 1795, in Mecklenburg County, North Carolina, and Warren Gamaliel Harding, our twenty-ninth leader, arrived at Blooming Grove, Ohio, on November 2, 1865. If you don't like either of them you also have your choice of Marie Antoinette and Daniel Boone, who seem to have had little or nothing in common except their birthday. Or you might concentrate on the fact that North and South Dakota were both admitted to the Union on November 2, 1889, the year after the Big Blizzard.

November 3

GUESS whose birthday *this* is—William Cullen Bryant's! I'm a little leery of William Cullen Bryant because I got into trouble in college for attributing to him the famous line, "The stag at eve had drunk his fill," which turned out to be by Sir Walter Scott, of all people. We had a whole volume of William Cullen Bryant at home containing a picture of a stag, and I always supposed it was the same stag. I still think there's something in it. Learning *Thanatopsis* by heart isn't the pleasantest way of spending one's formative years, either. I much preferred learning *To a Waterfowl*. It's so much shorter.

November 4

"DEAR SIR: What is the significance of the Postmaster's ruling that small alligators may be sent through the mails?
"Anxious"

To put the thing in a nutshell, this ruling means that small alligators may be sent through the mails. Personally, I hope it will result in a wider knowledge of reptiles in general and alligators in particular on the part of those who want that kind of knowledge. As herpetologists are fond of pointing out, reptiles are well worth knowing—unless you would rather know something else. Herpetologists are professors who know all about reptiles. They're about like other people, except that they are herpetologists.

Since you may receive some baby alligators at any moment, you ought to be told about the bright yellow bands they have across their backs. If these bands begin to fade and disappear, don't blame the alligators and don't accuse your friends of sending you an inferior grade. That always happens to alligators—seems too bad, but there it is. You needn't be afraid of baby alligators. They are usually very cute and tame until they grow older and see more of the world, when they act accordingly. Still, you never know an alligator until you've lived with it.

November 5

THOSE bright yellow flowers you saw in the woods the other day were probably witch hazel (*Hamamelis virginiana*), the latest of our deciduous shrubs to bloom. (No, I don't happen to know what deciduous means, so let's not go into it now.) The witch hazel waits until we think everything is over for the year and then bursts into bloom, as it doubtless in-tended to do all the time. Bursting is a sort of specialty with the witch hazel, for after the seeds are ripened—which takes until next autumn—they are forcibly ejected from the pod to a distance varying from five to forty feet, depending on the mood of the individual shrub and the say-so of the botanist who sees it. This is one of Mother Nature's provisions for in-suring the wider distribution of the witch hazel, but there seems to be a catch in it somewhere. While the witch hazel is turning itself inside out, popping its seeds forty feet, the seeds of calmer plants are picked up by birds and carried hun-dreds of miles. The joke seems to be on Mother Nature.

November 6

I HAVE just gone through a bit of mental torture, trying to figure the true inward significance of November 6 in song, story, and miscellaneous. What useful lessons can we draw from the events of this day; and if so, why? After delving into the past and adding up the results, I find myself at rather a loose end. It does strike me, however, that this world is a strange place indeed. November 6, 1793, marked the guillo-tining of Louis Philippe Joseph, Duc d'Orléans. Well, that was too bad, but they say it doesn't hurt. Besides, it was a long time ago, and he probably brought it on himself. Sometimes November 6 is fine, for John Philip Sousa was born on that day in 1856. And on this date in 1928 Herbert Hoover was elected President of the United States. Yes, it looks like a cold winter, all right.

ON NOVEMBER 7, 1811, General William Henry Harrison, who later became President of the United States, killed a lot of wild Indians at the Battle of Tippecanoe. That was in Indiana, but it was before my time. I think I may say that I was involved, however slightly, in the political fortunes of the general's grandson, President Benjamin Harrison, for when he was running for re-election in 1892 he came to our town and my mother led the Auburn Ladies' Glee Club in a

selection entitled *Ben Harrison Now Is Here*. The number ran, if memory serves:

> *Ben Harrison now is here,*
> *Ben Harrison now is here.*
> *Ben Harrison now, Ben Harrison **now**,*
> *Ben Harrison now is here.*

In the ensuing election President Harrison was badly defeated.

November 8

NOVEMBER 8, 1674, is an important date in literary history because it marks the passing of John Milton, a grand old man (except when he was crossed) and one of the best of the English poets. Milton wrote *Paradise Lost* and a number of other wonderful poems which were also fine. I would say more about Milton's work, but I'm a poetry-skipper myself. I don't like to boast, but I have probably skipped more poetry than any other person of my age and weight in this country —make it any other *two* persons. This doesn't mean that I hate poetry. I don't feel that strongly about it. It only means that those who wish to communicate with me by means of the written word must do so in prose. The only thing I hold against Milton is that he was a little too thick with Oliver Cromwell, and no friend of that old blighter can be a friend of mine.

November 9

I SUPPOSE you've noticed that the days are getting entirely too short lately. The sun sets at about 4:30 P.M. these days, and it will set earlier each day until the first part of December. Then, after two weeks, conditions will begin to improve, but it won't be until next April that things are anything like normal again. So what are you going to do with your long winter evenings this year? One authority advises: "Fill the home with the sunshine of love, and try to make every member of the household feel that home is the brightest spot on earth." I think I'll leave it at that. Anything I might add about home being the brightest spot on earth—I mean to say—Well, what do *you* think?

November 10

"DEAR SIR: Be nice and tell me your favorite recipe for *bouillabaisse*. I heard you're a whiz at it.

"*Brown Eyes*"

You heard nothing of the sort, *Brown Eyes*. You're only trying to draw me out because I hate French cooking. All I know is that *bouillabaisse* is a thin and decidedly odoriferous soup full of the bones and other débris of lobsters, eels, whiting, mullets, crayfish, and other lower vertebrates. If possible, it should also contain some racasses. Racasses are those little French fish which give to the celebrated *bouillabaisse* of Marseille that final *je ne sais quoi* which you can notice a block away if the wind is right. There are times, *Brown Eyes,* when I do not crave even one whiff of the *bouillabaisse* of Marseille. If you want the plain truth, I'd just as soon have a nice plate of tidewater.

November 11

OF ALL the fishes, the sticklebacks are the hardest to figure out. Some of the three-spined sticklebacks build nests; others don't. Some sticklebacks build their nests in the ends of rope left hanging in the water by children at picnics. Unfortunately, there are not enough ends of rope for all the sticklebacks.

The male stickleback has salmon-colored cheeks and blue and green sides. The female is duller, but around spawning time she brightens up and assumes a bridal dress. Both sexes have blue eyes.

The male is almost two inches long, but the female measures about two and a quarter. She never lets him forget it.

The Rogue Stickleback has any number of spines. You can never tell about Sticklebacks.

November 12

I ALWAYS like to know where people stand on King Canute, who died on November 12, 1035. It used to be said that King Canute carried his throne to the seashore and sat there in the erroneous belief that he was unwettable. They say now that he went to all that trouble as a rebuke to his flattering courtiers, who had been telling him that the ocean wouldn't dare touch such a big shot as the King of England, Norway, and Denmark. Either way, he got thoroughly soaked and made an awful chump of himself. In spite of historical research I'm

sticking to the earlier version on the ground that the plot of the other is too complicated for the net results and besides I don't believe it, anyway. I am firmly convinced that Canute actually *did* consider himself unwettable. I can't prove it, but there you are.

November 13

"DEAR SIR: Is it *au fait* to remark, after an introduction, 'I beg your pardon; I didn't quite catch the name'?
                                                     "Ambitious"

I wouldn't know, *Ambitious,* but I do feel it is slightly *non compos mentis.* Besides, you run the risk of saying it to somebody who goes practically mad at that particular remark. Such a person is likely to answer that he doesn't care whether you caught it or not. He may even do you bodily harm.

Personally, I try to be patient with those who didn't quite catch my name and wish to go into it more fully. I find, however, that when I explain the whole thing slowly, in all its letters and ramifications, they still seem unconvinced—or maybe that is their usual expression. I don't believe anything can be done about such people.

November 14

THIS is the birthday of Robert Fulton, the man who did not invent the steamboat. He invented a machine for making ropes and another for sawing marble, but not the steamboat. Robert Fulton was born November 14, 1765, at what is now Fulton, Pennsylvania. The steamboat was invented by two other fellows, mostly by John Fitch, in 1785, but nothing came of it. John Fitch died in 1798, flat broke and forgotten, and no towns were named after him. Robert Fulton studied all the plans and patents he could find, kept his eyes open, got plenty of financial backing, built the *Clermont* in 1807, and grew rich and famous. Some people are born lucky, and don't let anyone tell you different. Robert Fulton started out as a painter, but was converted to engineering by the Duke of Bridgewater, the father of the Bridgewater Canal, which is fifty feet wide and forty miles long, and altogether a very nice canal indeed.

November 15

IF YOU sat up after midnight on this date in 1934 you might have seen some Leonids, or meteors, left over from 1932 and 1933. Leonids come from the direction of the constellation Leo and are at their best every thirty-three years. I remember the shower of 1899 because I had a bag of hot salt tied around a terrible toothache and I finally had to have the tooth pulled. When meteors reach the earth they are called meteorites or aerolites. They never hit anybody you ever heard of before, so it's nothing to worry about.

November 16

"DEAR SIR: Is it *ee-ther* or *eye-ther*? I never know which to say and I feel that the time has come to face it.
"Louise"

I hesitate to speak freely on this matter, as I might say something I'd regret. Moreover, it is a problem that each of

us must solve for himself. It must come from inside, if you follow me. But I can give you a hint, *Louise*. Look about you,
listen to people talking, watch them at work and at play, and
if you want to be like the ones who say *eye-ther* I wouldn't
lay a straw in your way. Much the same line of reasoning applies to *to-may-to* and *to-mah-to*. Unless you come honestly
by it, have nothing to do with *to-mah-to*. I tried it once, and
I felt something awful for weeks afterwards. It simply isn't
in me.

November 17

YOU don't care a lot, probably, but on November 17, 1857,
Sir Colin Campbell accomplished the relief of Lucknow, saving the lives of many English men, women, and children.
For doing this he was raised to the peerage as Lord Clyde
and was therefore one jump better than he had been before.
The relief of Lucknow was part of the Indian Mutiny and
I think it had something to do with Sepoys, about which I
have always been very vague. If you are born in England you
instinctively know what a Sepoy is and what to do about it.
It's a good deal like knowing what an aspidistra is. The city
of Lucknow is in the district of Lucknow, which is in the
division of Lucknow, if that helps any.

November 18

"DEAR SIR: Are school children dumber than they used to
be, as somebody or other has just announced?
                                    "Pro Bono Publico"

Well, I collected a few data recently while coaching the

offspring of a friend in his grammar lesson, especially as to the technical divisions of the fairly simple sentence, "The man hit the dog." After expending a lot of eloquence on the component parts of sentences and making up several good ones as models, such as "John loves Mary" and "Mary loves John," I asked the lad to name me the subject of the sentence, "The man hit the dog." He said the subject was some trouble about a dog and stuck to it through thick and thin. I don't say he's dumb. But I do say he's different.

November 19

SPEAKING of dates, November 19 is important largely because Abraham Lincoln delivered his Gettysburg Address on this date in 1863. The Gettysburg Address is one of the noblest in our literature and is less than three hundred words long. I wish Lincoln had made it a little longer, for then nobody would have thought of engraving it on a penny. It's probably no use trying to understand why anyone would want to engrave the Gettysburg Address on a penny—we only know that there are people like that. There are people who whittle little wooden bird cages with little wooden balls inside them. There are people who collect first editions. In fact, there are all sorts of people.

November 20

"DEAR SIR: Whatever became of Vasco da Gama? Nobody ever seems to mention him any more. Or haven't *you* ever heard of him either?

"*Anxious*"

If you're trying to be nasty, *Anxious*, you've picked on the wrong person, because I happen to know all about Vasco da Gama. For one thing, it was on November 20, 1497, that he rounded the Cape of Good Hope and discovered the all-water route from Europe to India. I can assure you that Vasco's fame is as bright as ever in the right circles and that he is frequently mentioned by those with whom I converse—whom do you go around with, anyhow? What's more, Vasco da Gama was born in 1460 and died in 1524. So I never heard of him, eh?

November 21

IT SEEMS that on November 21, 1620, while the Pilgrim Fathers and Mothers were anchored in Provincetown Harbor after their famous trip to this country, they drew up the Mayflower Compact, which was a short constitution making them a body politic, whereas and notwithstanding. That is, the Pilgrim Fathers did this while the Pilgrim Mothers were busy

collecting the laundry for the Glorious Wash. The document was signed by forty-one of the seventy-five male passengers, thirteen of the remainder being minors and others nobody much. The most minor of all was Oceanus Hopkins, who was born on the way over. Oceanus has recieved little credit for this feat because Peregrine White arrived a month later and thus qualified as the first white child born in New England. It's pretty late in the day, but three cheers for Oceanus Hopkins!

November 22

THIS is positively the last day for Scorpio children until next year. Persons born tomorrow and until midnight of December 22 will be under the sign of Sagittarius, if you believe in signs. Most of them will have their ups and downs, but they may get along all right if they Keep Smiling. The more intelligent among them will have spells when they will be unable to do this. Sagittarius persons know things by intuition, but they often find that some of it isn't so. Celebrated Sagittarians include Mark Twain, Benedictus de Spinoza, Andrew Carnegie, St. Francis Xavier, Fay Bainter, Ludwig van Beethoven, Minnie Maddern Fiske, Newton D. Baker, Louisa May Alcott, Christina Rossetti, Thomas Carlyle, Paracelsus, and Lillian Russell.

November 23

THIS is the birthday of Abigail Smith Adams, the only lady, so far as I know, who ever became the wife of one President of the United States and the mother of another. Abigail Smith was born November 23, 1744, at Weymouth, Massachusetts. She married John Adams in 1764 and died in 1818, leaving John Quincy Adams and several other children to increase and multiply the Adams family. The Adams family now includes perfect droves of persons noted for their high degree of civic integrity, social consciousness, and miscellaneous brain power. And if you ask me they got most of it from the Smith family, for Abigail Smith Adams appears to have been quite a lot brighter than her husband. Speaking of families, one of our leading citizens once remarked that he would rather know the Jukeses than the Adamses, because he believed they had more fun in them, but he must have been joking.

November 24

ON NOVEMBER 24, 1815, at eight o'clock in the morning, guess who was born at Bamborough, Northumberland. Grace Darling, that's who! Yes, she's the girl who had something to do with a wreck, and whatta girl! One terrible day in 1838, when Grace was twenty-two, the steamer *Forfarshire,* bound from Hull to Dundee, was smashed on some rocks near Longstone Light, where none other than our Grace was watching right through the storm. So right then and there Grace and her father rowed out in a gale of wind and rescued the nine survivors against odds of about a thousand to one. You can hardly blame the old sailor, clinging to the rock, who cried out: "For the Lord's sake, there's a lassie coming!" Queen Victoria sent her a present of fifty pounds, and all England went mad over her, but poor Grace was naturally frail and she died at the age of twenty-five. They don't come any better than Grace.

November 25

SOME people find it hard to believe, but a ling once produced 28,361,000 eggs. A 17-pound turbot contained 9,161,-000 eggs, and more than 280,000 eggs have been taken from a ½-pound perch.

A codfish often lays more than nine million eggs. Even a goldfish can be counted on for 2,000 to 70,000 eggs a year.

A sunfish sometimes lays 300 million eggs. What are they trying to prove?

November 26

"DEAR SIR: How big is Halley's comet and how fast can it go? I missed it a couple of years ago and I'm just crazy to see it the next time.

"Blue Eyes"

You must have your comets mixed, *Blue Eyes.* Halley's comet last appeared in 1910. I was sleeping at the time so I never saw it, but a great many people did—or said they did, which is a slightly different thing. Naturally, I never measured it myself, but a fellow who ought to know tells me that its head was approximately 161,000 miles in diameter and its tail exactly 27,800,000 miles long as observed by a friend of his. This makes it only a medium-sized comet, as comets go, not nearly so large as you might think from all the talk about it, year in and year out.

My informant states that this comet travels about 100,000 miles per hour, at least part of the time, but it doesn't give you that impression. Nor does it swoop from one end of the heavens to another or whiz around in circles like a fiery dragon having a fit, if that's what you're expecting. The head looks like an ordinary star, only fuzzier, and the tail is more or less of a shapeless blur. I hear the photographers have to touch it up some to make even a decent picture.

I gather that Mr. Halley, who got his name attached to it by calculating its orbit in 1704 and accurately predicting its return, was no slouch at public relations. He certainly worked up a lot of excitement about it. Of course he was good, too, as you have to be in that business. If you predict the return of a comet and it doesn't return, you look pretty silly.

November 27

THIS day in history is only so-so. On November 27, 1520, Ferdinand Magellan entered the Pacific Ocean by sailing through the Strait of Magellan, only it wasn't named that until later. I would think more of Magellan if he had actually rounded the Horn instead of overlooking Tierra del Fuego altogether. Sneaking through the Strait of Magellan is a good deal like cutting second base. And November 27, 1703, was the climax of the Big Storm in England, when $10,000,-000 property damage was done in London alone and the Bishop of Wells and his wife were killed in their bed by a stack of falling chimneys. The Hoosac Tunnel was completed November 27, 1873—there's something constructive, at any rate. History can't be working at top speed *all* the time.

November 28

DAYDREAMS can be very charming things. And they're useful too. The professors say that daydreams are a valuable part of our constitution, letting off steam as they do and sort of

ministering to minds in need of a recess—only don't do it on the boss's time. My waking phantasies today have been mostly concerned with that noble vegetable, the pumpkin. Pumpkins are generally classified as fruit, but not by me. They look, taste, and act like vegetables, and for me that makes them vegetables. Pumpkins are rich in carbohydrates, fairly full of minerals, and moderately provided with Vitamins A and B. You can bake, boil, or steam pumpkins, but they were originally intended for pie, and I see no reason to go against nature.

November 29

ON THIS date in 1929 Commander Richard E. Byrd, accompanied by Bernt Balchen and two other fellows, flew over the South Pole and returned safely to their base at Little America, astronomers at Paris, Cordoba, and Pasadena saw some more sun spots, Mount Pelée threatened to erupt, and Pola Negri applied for a divorce from Prince Serge Mdivani. For violating the liquor laws of the nation a lady in Muncie, Indiana, got a suspended six months' sentence on information supplied by her neighbors, who had listened in on the telephone. It seems that people would call up the lady and order half a red chicken or half a white chicken, but that didn't fool the neighbors for a moment. And it was twenty-six degrees below zero in Three River Falls, Minnesota. I often wonder why we don't all move to a nice warm climate. If the monkeys can do it, *we* can do it.

November 30

JONATHAN SWIFT, one of your favorite authors, was born in Dublin on November 30, 1667. He was a very bright man but somewhat cantankerous, and he kept getting worse. In 1726 he published the first two parts of *Gulliver's Travels*, all about the Lilliputians, who are only one-twelfth as big as we are, and the Brobdingnagians, who are twelve times as big as we are. Almost everybody loved *Gulliver's Travels*, and it became a best-seller, but some of the critics were on the fence —you know how critics are. An Irish bishop said the book was full of improbable lies and that for his part he hardly believed a word of it. And Doctor Samuel Johnson ate some more mutton and announced: "When you have once thought of big men and little men, it is easy to do the rest." That's about what he *would* say.

DECEMBER

December 1

I'M NOT so sure that the fault, Dear Brutus, is in ourselves that we keep putting things off. I won't say that it's in our stars, either, but something's always turning up to ruin our chances of fame and fortune; at least it's that way with me. Here it's December already, and I had vowed to finish my Great American Drama before Christmas at the latest. I finished the first act a number of years ago and it seems as though I haven't had a minute since that I could call my own. A notation in my diary for December 1, 1933, shows that I planned to start work on the second act the next morning without fail. Well, the next morning I got up with a terrible cold and was practically in bed for the next two weeks. Maybe I keep putting this off because I'm not quite sure whether the *first* act is any good.

December 2

SIR Francis Bacon has said, among many other things, that the age of the salmon exceeds not 10 years. Pure rubbish, Sir Francis!

There seems to be some doubt these days about the parent-stream theory—that salmon return to spawn in the stream in which they were hatched. Jordan says they do no such thing. I have a feeling some do and some don't.

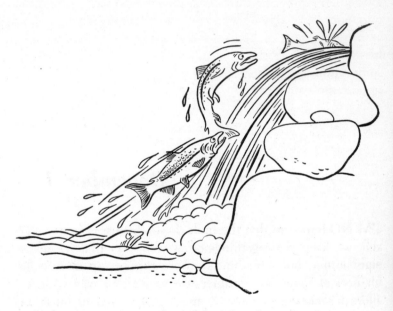

At the proper time male and female salmon head upstream, have a number of small salmon, and die. All baby salmon are orphans at an early age, but they don't think anything of it. It happens in the best of salmon families.

Salmon ascend rivers with strongly running waters and jump numerous falls—but usually not more than 10 feet at a jump. Although salmon start up the Niagara River for a short stretch, they don't continue on. They seem to know there's a catch in it.

December 3

SEEMS that this is the birthday of Gilbert Stuart, who painted that portrait of George Washington; General George Brinton McClellan, once Commander-in-Chief of the Army of the Potomac; Ellen Henrietta Richards, pioneer female chemist; and of all people, Samuel Crompton, inventor of the spinning mule. And by spinning mule I do not mean the spinning jenny or the cotton gin—those were different things altogether, although I can't say at the moment just wherein the difference lay. Samuel Crompton was born December 3, 1753, at Firwood, near Bolton-le-Moors, Lancashire. He produced his spinning mule about 1779, and died poor. Since then the spinning mule has been greatly improved until now it is said to be quite wonderful, if you care for those things.

December 4

IF YOU *must* celebrate somebody's birth today, you could yell for Thomas Carlyle, who arrived at Ecclefechan, in Annandale, December 4, 1795. I have never been able to enjoy his *French Revolution* because of its jumpiness; I can't stand authors who try to pump up excitement by writing about history in the present tense. *Sartor Resartus* is simply unreadable, and for me that always sort of spoils a book. Carlyle once remarked: "Americans! Forty million people, mostly fools." Yes, and what I know about him! He was a cranky old codger with indigestion and auditory hyperesthesia. He built himself a soundproof room on top of his house so that he couldn't hear his neighbor's roosters. When he was in it he could still hear the roosters but the roosters couldn't hear him so it did some good, anyway.

December 5

ON THIS date in 1839 there was great excitement in the Custer family, at New Rumley, Ohio, and the baby was named George Armstrong Custer. George grew up, went to West Point, graduated at the foot of a class of thirty-four, and became a general in the Civil War, doing great work at Bull Run, Gettysburg, Appomattox, and other places. Later he began fighting the Indians out west and he and his entire command of two hundred and sixty-four men were massacred by Chief Sitting Bull at the Battle of Big Horn, Montana, June 25, 1876. At least the encyclopedia calls it the Battle of Big Horn, Montana. I was brought up to call it Custer's Last Stand. Sitting Bull was killed in 1890 when some of his friends tried to rescue him from some Indian policemen. He was shot in the back by Red Tomahawk and Lieutenant Bullhead. Sitting Bull caused a little trouble sometimes, but by and large he was a good Indian.

December 6

"DEAR SIR: I am very fond of tripe, but my husband refuses to touch it. Do you think he loves me?
"Distracted"

You came to me just in time, *Distracted*. Unless you watch yourself, I'm afraid you're on the way out. Your husband simply isn't the type, as you should have gathered long ago. Tripe-lovers are born, not made, and no amount of argument is going to change that fundamental law of nature. This world is full of people who are ready and willing to eat tripe, *Distracted*—why pick on your husband? I suggest that you give a series of tripe luncheons to persons who share your point of view, so that you will be ready to greet your mate with a smile and a good steak when he returns from the office. This bit of advice also holds good for fried bananas, if not more so.

P. S.—Sure he loves you, but there *is* a limit.

December 7

I'M NOT a bit surprised that our high school students consider black cats unlucky, as discovered by Professors Caldwell and Lundeen of Teachers College, Columbia University —although I, personally, have found Maltese cats much worse. What I want to see blasted is the outrageous and abominable superstition that cows eat buttercups and that this improves their milk. An old friend tells me that cows simply hate buttercups and never eat them, even when pasturage is scarce. I believe him, because I once ate a buttercup and it was extremely bitter. Since then I have confined my flower-eating mostly to nasturtiums, with here and there maybe a rose leaf. So if cows don't eat buttercups how can eating buttercups improve their milk? Why not look into *that*?

December 8

YOU may as well get it straight about the cotton gin, once for all. The cotton gin separates the seeds from the cotton fibers, and that is more important than it sounds. It used to take one man ten hours to separate three pounds of seeds from one pound of cotton fibers, and Eli Whitney found out about it while visiting the South. I'm afraid most of us would have said: "Oh, let the old seeds stay where they are, what do I care?" But Eli Whitney flew right at it and invented the cotton gin in 1793, and it did the work of a thousand men. He never made much money out of it, for people stole his ideas and the courts were against him, but he made a lot afterwards by manufacturing rifles for the government. By the way, Eli Whitney was born at Westborough, Massachusetts, on December 8, 1765.

December 9

SOCRATES was considered to be one of the greatest thinkers

of his time. He said that Happiness is Virtue and Virtue is Happiness, and therefore no man will do wrong if he can help it, for if he does wrong he will not be virtuous and therefore he will not be happy, since Happiness is Virtue and Virtue is Happiness.

The Socratic Method consisted mostly of asking questions. Socrates would listen to people talking and then he would ask them exactly what they meant by what they had said and whether they knew what they were talking about. This was embarrassing for the people, because they had not meant much of anything. They were just talking. If they had known what they were talking about, they would not have been talking. Then Socrates would prove to them that they had no sense whatever. He seems to have thought this would please them. As you probably know, he was forced to drink hemlock, in 399 B.C. At his trial he denied that he was a wise man, but nobody would believe him.

December 10

ALFRED BERNHARD NOBEL, Swedish chemist and engineer, inventor of dynamite and founder of the Nobel prizes, passed away on December 10, 1896. Of the five yearly prizes, each worth about $30,000 these days, I have always been most interested in the one awarded to the person who shall have produced in the field of literature the most distinguished work of an idealist tendency, and I supposed I could tell you all about the winners. Somewhat to my surprise, I find that I know nothing whatever about Karl Gjellerup and Henrik Pontoppidan, two Danish gentlemen who shared the cash in 1917. During 1917 I must have been skipping literature of an idealist tendency, or maybe I was busy trying not to get blown up with dynamite. But you can't fool me on Henrik Sienkiewicz, who copped the money in 1905. He wrote *Quo Vadis?*, the favorite book of my childhood days unless it was *Ben Hur*.

December 11

"DEAR SIR: Whatever became of Pluto, the fairly new planet that used to be in the newspapers all the time?
                                                                    "Admirer"

I fancied you were kidding at first, *Admirer,* and I was going to come right back at you with a still funnier question, if I could have thought of it. I had picked up the idea somewhere that Pluto was a phony, but it seems I was wrong. An astronomical friend tells me that Pluto is all right. He says that Pluto is now about as popular as Uranus and Neptune, although it will probably never be as popular as Venus, Jupiter, and Mars, which we can all see and keep track of— we can see Saturn, too, but somehow it has never been popular. Pluto's mean distance from the sun is about 3,671,000,-000 miles, or about forty times our mean distance from the sun, so it's really too far away to do much good. It was only discovered in 1930, though, so something may come of it yet.

December 12

THIS IS the birthday of Gustave Flaubert, a great French novelist, who arrived at Rouen on December 12, 1821. He was famous for always seeking *le mot juste* in everything he wrote, even if it took weeks, and to me that merely means that he had a harder time than most authors in finding the right word —nothing to brag of, I'd say. For years I worried terribly because I didn't like Flaubert's *Madame Bovary,* so I read it again not long ago and found out why—it isn't very good. But *Salammbô* is fine. Of course it may be that I like novels only when they are full of elephants and Carthaginians and heathen goddesses and costumes that positively clank with jewelry. I may add that I once saw Blanche Walsh in a dramatization of *Salammbô* and I never enjoyed a show more, unless it was *The Last Days of Pompeii* in fireworks. Give me the grand manner every time.

December 13

DECEMBER 13 is one of those days that don't stand out in history to any sensational extent. Still, Heinrich Heine, German poet, was born December 13, 1797, and he can't be beaten in his line. And Phillips Brooks, distinguished Episcopalian bishop, started life on the same date in 1835—and a fine bishop he was, too. Also, General Robert E. Lee defeated General Ambrose E. Burnside at Fredericksburg, December 13, 1862. That pretty well cleans up what I know about December 13, except that last year at this time I had a common cold, same as I have now, and that I was trying seventeen sure cures instead of the nineteen I'm trying now. So today is no July 4, but I have a feeling that lots of things happened on December 13 that never got into print. Let us hope so.

December 14

YOUR old friend Henry of Navarre, who later became Henry IV of France, was born December 14, 1553. He was the one who said "It is my wish that every peasant may have meat for dinner every day of the week and a chicken in his pot every Sunday." The peasants didn't get it, but they were so pleased that they called Henry *le Roi de la poule au pot,* or *the king of the chicken in the pot.* Henry was a ladies' man of the first order of merit, but he once said something rather dubious about Queen Elizabeth. When Elizabeth was far gone in years the English ambassador showed him a portrait of the old girl and he remarked, according to the chroniclers, "that he had never seen the like." Naturally, the ambassador took it as a compliment. What else could he do?

December 15

"DEAR SIR: Just what is this new suspense novel we're getting these days? How would you define it?

"Unnerved"

The so-called suspense story, or suspense novel, of current commerce has been defined in several ways, none of them really satisfactory. One of our smartest mystery editors says it is a crime story in which you know who killed whom right away. You are not held in doubt as to the identity of the murderer through a whole book, as you are in the old-fashioned detective tale or in the ordinary whodunit. Thus a suspense story would appear to be a crime story with the suspense removed, or a mystery with its raison d'être, if you follow me, yanked out and thrown away in the first chapter.

Now what does that leave the suspense author for the rest of his story? Plenty. Characterization, as we of the old school used to call it. Writing, as such. There is no reason on earth, except one into which we need not go at the moment, why he cannot proceed to compose another *Crime and Punishment.* How did the killer get that way? (This point is left somewhat vague in Dostoievsky's great work. In my opinion, the fellow was just no good.) Why was I ever born, Babushka? Will the cops catch him? Certainly they will. What's more, suspense authors do make efforts in all these directions. But are these questions as interesting to the patrons of the lending libraries as the old central problem of mystery: Who dunit? Unfortunately, no.

This mystery editor states that the fans are restive under the new suspense order. They are screaming for the dear old clues. They don't wanna be told in the first chapter.

Meanwhile, the word "suspense" is having a time for itself.

December 16

TAKE the head of a camel, the body of a deer, the wool of a sheep, and the neigh of a horse, and what do you have?

As any Patagonian child will tell you, you have a guanaco,

a sort of cousin of the llama, which is smaller, less graceful, and altogether a poor relation.

Guanacos run wild throughout the southern part of South America, from Peru to Cape Horn. They live in herds of six to thirty guanacos. When several of them come upon a Patagonian hunter, they stand motionless and gaze intently at him, then move on a few yards, to give him a better view. At that point they turn around and look some more. They can't believe their eyes.

The Ona Indians of Tierra del Fuego, who were not very bright themselves, used to club the guanaco to death. They ate guanaco and dressed in guanaco fur. Today the Onas are pretty well washed up.

December 17

"DEAR SIR: Please give me the rest of the Whittier poem that goes this way:

> *Bob-o'-link, Bob-o'-link*
> *Spink, spank, spink.*

Don't you love Whittier?

> *"Anxious"*

Try to be a little more careful how you bandy people's names about. *Robert of Lincoln,* which contains the lines you quote, was written by William Cullen Bryant and not by John Greenleaf Whittier. You should be able to obtain a copy without much trouble, but I will not be a party to it. I have done enough for that poem. I was once scheduled to speak it in school and I had to come down with a fake attack of whooping cough to avoid it. I knew that if I spoke that thing I could never look the other children in the face again, and my opinion hasn't changed. Personally, I think the worst line in the poem—I might almost say in *any* poem—is

Chee, chee, chee.

Oh, I nearly forgot. This is Whittier's birthday. He was born December 17, 1807, in Haverhill, Massachusetts.

December 18

KARL Maria Friedrich Ernst von Weber, German composer, was born December 18, 1786. He wrote several operas, including *Der Freischütz,* but he is perhaps best known to us lowbrows for his piano piece, *Invitation to the Dance,* every note of which is but too familiar to anybody whose sister ever took lessons. Although *Invitation to the Dance* can pall with frequent repetition, there are ways of making it much less depressing. For instance, take the first page very slowly, very *con espressione,* as if butter wouldn't melt in your mouth, then tackle the second movement, *allegro vivace,* with every ounce of your strength. Above all, get some speed into the main, or grind organ, waltz theme—don't give your audience time to think. The trouble is that the darn thing goes on practically forever. I don't know how you'd get around that.

December 19

ANOTHER gadget that I can't understand is the interferometer, an extremely delicate instrument used for measuring small differences in wave length—so small, in fact, that you wouldn't believe it. I mention this because Albert A. Michelson, who invented the thing, was born December 19, 1852, in Strelno, Germany; and also because Professor Michelson was a teacher of mine, in a way. At least he once explained the fine points of his interferometer to Professor Robert A. Millikan's Physics I class at the University of Chicago, but it left me about where I was. Professor Michelson was a great teacher, though, when he had something to work on. At that time he was head of the Physics Department and I was what you might call the foot. I was pretty proud when Professor Michelson measured the diameter of Betelgeuse in 1920, and found out it was 260,000,000 miles.

December 20

"DEAR SIR: Will you kindly tell me how the days of the week got their names?

"Anonymous"

No, I will not. I have gone to the trouble of reading eleven encyclopedias on the subject, and about all I got is that the Mayas had some days named *Imix, Ik,* and *Ix* and the Chinese some others named *Ping* and *Ting* and the ancient Babylonians didn't seem to know *what* they were doing about it. Fortunately, an aunt of mine once told me that Thursday is Thursday because the Scandinavians had a day called Thor's day—if that will help you. Thor was the god of thunder, but it doesn't seem to thunder any more on Thursday than on Friday. I'm afraid you asked the wrong person, *Anonymous*. I go all blooey when I start reading about the calendar and how it happened.

December 21

THIS is Forefathers' Day for those whose ancestors came over in the *Mayflower,* and a great day for the rest of us, too. For on December 21, 1620, the Pilgrims came to a large bowlder on the coast of Massachusetts, and went ashore and started New England. They called the place New Plymouth (later just Plymouth) and the bowlder Plymouth Rock, and you can still see it by going there. It is said that the first person to step on Plymouth Rock was Mary Chilton, who afterwards married John Winslow and had ten children and lived mostly in Boston. Mrs. Felicia Dorothea Hemans (*née* Browne), who wrote that poem about the Pilgrims arriving on a stern and rockbound coast, was not there at the time. She wasn't born until 1793.

December 22

WHETHER you like it or not, winter is beginning, because we've come to the winter solstice. Putting it simply, the winter solstice is either the point in the ecliptic at which the sun is farthest south of the celestial equator or the time at which the sun reaches said point—you get the main drift? At any rate, it will be winter until we come to the vernal equinox, but you don't have to worry about that for a while. A great many poets have written in praise of winter. And the same poets have written in praise of spring, summer, autumn, or anything else that has a ready market value to people who like poetry. Personally, I think winter is a mistake.

December 23

IF YOU were born between now and January 20, you are under the Sign of Capricorn, the Goat, but don't blame me, blame the astrologers. Natives of Capricorn, as they are called, are generally sure-footed and frequently handsome. They always know whether they are going north or south without looking at the street numbers or asking a policeman. They often succeed as soldiers, sailors, orators, poets, Presidents of the United States, housewives, woolen merchants, and provision dealers. Capricorn persons of the past and present include William Ewart Gladstone, Eva LeGallienne, Kit Carson, Matthew Arnold, Clara Barton, Peter Ilyitch Tschaikovsky, Howard Chandler Christy, Woodrow Wilson, Marshal Joffre, Stephen Decatur, Marcus Tullius Cicero, Lina Cavalieri, Ethan Allen, Mrs. Calvin Coolidge, and Paul Revere.

December 24

"DEAR SIR: What do you think of a husband who simply won't touch fried eggplant?

"Mrs. X"

I think he might go far. You will generally find that a man who is right in these small matters is a man to be trusted. I am sure he doesn't bother with steamed summer squash, either, and that he considers okra in any form a waste of time and okra. He may toy with an artichoke now and then, but it is only to keep peace in the family. Not that fried eggplant is particularly horrid or frightful. It is not a thing to arouse frantic hatred in every right-thinking citizen, like pineapple pie. It just doesn't matter, and that's almost worse.

December 25

SIR Isaac Newton was one of those persons who lost out on two sets of presents because they were born on Christmas. He arrived in 1642, and I wish I could give you the real facts about that apple. Some say that Sir Isaac did *not* think up his theory of gravitation while watching an apple fall from a tree,

and others say that they could show you the very tree from which the apple fell. Apple or no apple, I have always admired the great man's comment on the passing of Roger Cotes, a brilliant young mathematician cut off in his prime in 1716. Said Sir Isaac, then nearing seventy-four and as full of honors as one can well be: "If Mr. Cotes had lived, we should have known something." You don't hear Grade B scientists talking like that.

December 26

IN A certain oration before both houses of Congress on December 26, 1799, there occurred a phrase so striking and so quotable that everybody noticed it. The speaker was General Henry Lee, better known as Light Horse Harry Lee; the speech was about George Washington, who had died a few days before, and you've already guessed the phrase, which was "First in war, first in peace, and first in the hearts of his countrymen." Few remember what else Light Horse Harry said, but it doesn't matter a lot, because that was enough for one speech. Light Horse Harry Lee was a Princeton man, class of 1773. During the Revolution he won a gold medal for his attack on Paulus Hook, New Jersey, and later he was Governor of Virginia, suh! What is more, ladies and gentlemen, he was the father of General Robert E. Lee, and that was no mean accomplishment, either.

December 27

ON DECEMBER 27, 1822, there was born a little Frenchman who looked like all other little Frenchmen but wasn't. He seemed rather stupid in school, rating only "mediocre" in chemistry. His trouble was not dumbness, however, but genius. He soon struck his stride, and his discoveries about microbes made a big difference in everything, from beer and vinegar to silkworms, sheep, cattle, mad dogs, and men. Pasteur was probably the greatest Frenchman who ever lived, unless you're a Napoleon fan—personally, I'm not.

The French people once voted on the matter and Pasteur won, with Napoleon second, and Victor Hugo third—that's how *they* felt about it. There are still lots of people who don't believe in germs. There are also people who don't believe in Niagara Falls, and if it keeps falling apart the way it's been doing lately, they'll be right.

December 28

"DEAR SIR: Please tell me how to increase my vocabulary so that I can talk more like the highbrows do.

"*Ambitious*"

Your use of the word *like* is far from perfect, *Ambitious*. For reasons into which I am pretty sure it would be useless to go just now, either change the *like* to *as* or omit the *do*. Your problem, as I see it, is rather to try to get some faint glimmering about the words in your present vocabulary than to fly to others that you know not of, if I may put it that way. Shakespeare got along nicely with only 23,000 words and you ought to do with less. For one thing, you might start an investigation of the difference between *shall* and *will*, and if you find out anything definite, let me know.

December 29

WILLIAM EWART GLADSTONE, four times Prime Minister of England, was born in Liverpool on December 29, 1809. Unlike some great men, he showed early promise of leadership. When he was promoted to the fifth form at Eton he treated his schoolmates to an ode condemning their barbarous custom of cutting the tails off pigs at the Ash Wednesday fairs. So the next Ash Wednesday the boys cut off more pigtails than ever, and left three fresh ones at Gladstone's door, with a Latin inscription telling him a thing or two about people who don't like to have the tails cut off pigs. Gladstone didn't get along with Queen Victoria, either, but he was the Grand Old Man just the same.

December 30

"DEAR SIR: If squirrels store up nuts for the winter, why don't they eat them instead of begging me for peanuts all the time?

"Annoyed"

You should be more patient with the squirrels, my friend. It is true that they follow certain people the minute they see them, but there must be a reason for this. You probably have a kind face. Squirrels do store up nuts for the winter, but they seem to forget where they stored them. Or it may be that they had no intention of eating the nuts at all, and therefore do not *care* where they stored them. Perhaps they merely have an idea that storing nuts is the main function of a squirrel and do not go into the matter more deeply. Still, you never know how squirrels feel about things. That's why they're squirrels.

December 31

ONE thing we are spared in this country is the celebration of Hogmanay, which is a Scotch name for the last day of the year and also for the small oatmeal cakes appertaining to same. On the morning of December 31 the Scotch children dress themselves in sheets and go from house to house soliciting the cakes or other food with the cry:

> Hogmanay,
> Trollolay,
> Gie's o' your white bread and nane o' your grey.

If this doesn't work they will try this one:

> Get up, good wife, and shake your feathers,
> And dinna think that we are beggars;
> For we are bairns come out to play;
> Get up and gie's our hogmanay.

I have a feeling that the children who do this are a little too quaint for their own good. Over here we'd call them problem children.

Index